Ros~ ~.~~~~
*in collaboration with* Rita María Hernández

# Blank Page

*Stories of hope and triumph from human trafficking survivors*

***grafohouse***

GUADALAJARA, JALISCO, MEXICO

BOTHELL, WA, USA

**Blank Page**
© 2020 Rosi Orozco

Published by Grafo House Publishing
Guadalajara, Jalisco, Mexico; grafohouse.com

In association with Jaquith Creative, a creative and literary agency
Bothell, Washington, USA, jaquithcreative.com

hardbound ISBN 978-1-949791-43-3
paperback ISBN 978-1-949791-20-4
ebook ISBN 978-1-949791-21-1

Library of Congress Control Number: 9781949791204

Originally published in Spanish under the title *Hoja en Blanco*.

For more information about this title, including bulk sales, please email
info@grafohouse.com

Book design by Nacho Huizar, nachohuizar.com

First Edition
23 22 21 20    1 2 3 4

*For God, my husband Alex, and my family,*
*for their support and unconditional love;*
*for all the trafficking victims and survivors;*
*and for our allies who are so crucial in this fight.*

# Praise and endorsements

"*Blank Page* is a captivating example of human trafficking survivors reclaiming their story. Having covered stories in places like La Merced and Tlaxcala,
I've seen firsthand the dire circumstances many of
the victims in Orozco's book often experience. *Blank
Page* shows that even out of the darkest depths of
human trafficking, survivors can still find the
strength to regain their freedom and, in the process,
rewrite the narrative of their own lives."

**Leif Coorlim**
Executive Editor of the CNN Freedom Project

"Rosi Orosco has been a pioneer in helping us understand that we can make a difference in the world
in the fight against human trafficking. She has survived death threats, persecutions, and press attacks.
Rosi is a Jerome in every sense of the word. This
book will change your life."

**Dr. Cindy Jacobs**
Author, international speaker, and cofounder
of Generals International

"The mission of Innocents at Risk since 2005 has been to educate the public in the US and around the world about the horrific issue of human trafficking. Innocents at Risk has worked with a vast number of partners, including Rosi Orozco, in the fight to end the trafficking of women and children. Rosi has dedicated her life to helping rescue and restore the lives of over 300 girls and boys in Mexico. As founder and director of Innocents at Risk, I have met many of these young survivors of trafficking who are now educated and successful in their careers. Rosi Orozco has now given us a gift by putting her knowledge and experiences in an excellent book, *Blank Page*. The book consists of stories of survivors of human trafficking, shelters, and NGOs that Rosi has worked with in Mexico. The book also contains information about the scope of the global trafficking problem, the strategies and the tactics that traffickers use to lure innocent girls and boys, and ways to prevent this horrific evil. *Blank Pages* is a brilliant book that is a must read for everyone!"

**Deborah S. Sigmund**
Founder, Executive Director, Innocents at Risk

"We all want to put an end to this scourge of human trafficking, but Rosi Orozco and Rita Hernandez are doing exactly that every day. I have seen them intervene in the lives of many survivors, rescuing them, caring for them, and helping them launch into a bright new future. The stories you read in *Blank Page* are powerful because they are being told firsthand by the ones who made them possible. I have also met many of the survivors in these stories, and the transformation is real and lasting. If you want to be inspired to keep fighting for justice and freedom for the enslaved, then you will want to read this book."

**Del Chittim**
Chief Operating Officer, Rescue: Freedom International

"Human trafficking is one of the fastest-growing crimes in the world today, and it will continue to be so until the world opens its eyes to what is happening. In this book, Rosi Orozco will open your eyes! As you read these true stories—stories Rosi was personally involved in—of those who have been kidnapped, trafficked, and rescued, you will learn what you need to do in order to be part of the solution. You will also be inspired as you learn of victims who became survivors and ultimately thrivers. This book is a tribute to the human spirit and its ability to overcome."

**Tim Ballard**
Founder, Operation Underground Railroad

"Two things are necessary to eradicate the crime against humanity known as prostitution: prevention through laws inspired by the Nordic model (which, for the first time in history, penalizes the consumer and not the victim), and the rehabilitation of victims through a protocol that reintegrates them into society. Rosi Orozco is an example of both. Her rehabilitation protocol may be the best model I have ever seen, because not only does she give survivors the spiritual strength to recover their own dignity and freedom as people, she also strives to provide them with a professional degree, a dignified job, and a roof over their heads to build their own family. We can describe this protocol, which has saved more than three hundred precious young women, by paraphrasing the words of Saint Peter, that where evil abounded, good, dignity, liberty, companionship, and friendship now abound much more."

**Marcelo Sanchez Sorondo**
Chancellor of the Pontifical Academy of the Sciences

"Rosi Orozco is a worldwide leader in the fight against human trafficking. I deeply admire her work to clothe with human rights thousands of women and girls who have been stripped of those rights."

**Mabel Lozano**
Film director and author of the book and movie *El Proxeneta* (The Pimp)

viii

"This book is an intimate insight into one of the greatest atrocities of our lifetime: human trafficking. A fierce advocate for those enslaved, Rosi Orozco has risked her life in the service of helping those trapped in forced prostitution. In *Blank Page*, Rosi encourages victims whose voices were once silenced to tell their stories boldly—and to dare to live out new ones. It is a book not only of hardship but also of joy; and most poignantly, of the resilience of the human heart."

**Lisa Kristine**
Humanitarian photographer

"*Blank Page* is an incredible book that tells the stories of more than the few women mentioned within its pages. The lives described in this book represent the nameless millions of men, women, and children who are currently being held against their will across our world. Rosi brings her readers into a world that most of us would like to believe does not exist. But it does. I have seen girls like the ones written about within the pages of this book. They are surviving in horrific conditions in every country of the world and most likely even within your neighborhood. Rosi's life of compassion and courage to go into that world and make a way for others to be free from it will challenge and inspire you to want to be part of doing whatever it takes to stop human trafficking. One person can make a difference, and Rosi Orozco is proving that."

**JoAnne Ramos**
Churchome Missions Pastor

"This powerful book documents the journey of human trafficking victims. The stories are captivating and shocking: the lives of 'the forgotten,' those who were dangerously close to disappearing as if they had never existed at all, blank pages of humanity. Unknown, brutalized and violently abused, they were stripped of their innocence and their freedom; ignored, except for the intervention of Rosi Orozco. Rosi's brave commitment has changed the lives of these victims and pointed them toward a future of trust, hope, and restoration of their dignity. She is a champion for human rights. *Blank Page* is a must-read book."

**Blanquita Cullum**
Former director of US International Broadcasting, an alliance dedicated to ending human trafficking

"*Blank Page* is required reading for everyone who wants to see the world liberated from modern slavery. Rosi Orozco shows us the tragic reality that millions of people are living today and, at the same time, invites us to be part of the change. With every story Rosi shares, you will find that hope is possible for our world."

**Andres Spyker**
Más Vida Mexico

# Contents

*More than survivors, now successful young women and activists. From left to right: Neli, Madaí, Mixi, and Karla Jacinto with Rosi Orozco.*

# Introduction:
# Why a blank page?

**When victims of** human trafficking arrive at a shelter, they are usually in a state of total devastation. Their course of life has been completely and cruelly destroyed: their dignity has been stomped on, their dreams taken away, their free will broken. Because of this, one of the first things we do at our shelters is give them a blank sheet of paper. Then we encourage them to remember the dreams they used to have and write them on the page. For many, it takes days, weeks, months, or even years before they can dream again, before they can remember the things they had hoped to achieve in life. They frequently believe they aren't capable or even worthy of achieving those goals.

A blank page is a space to write a new story, one in which there is no more shame, no more pain, no more tormenting memories; there is only the hope of tomorrow and a letting go of the past to focus on what is ahead.

I will never forget one instance when we picked up two trafficking victims, both young boys, from the Mexican city of Torreón, Coahuila. We decided to give them their blank pages while we were flying home. During the flight, we spoke about the significance of this page: how it symbolized that at this very moment they were leaving their past behind so they could start over. Months later, we received their tender, handwritten response: "Thank you for my blank page." Today, these boys are living a completely new and different story.

In 2015 my team and I launched a campaign designed by the well-known publicist Clemente Cámara called "Hoja en Blanco" (Blank Page), with the goal of increasing the general public's solidarity with human trafficking victims. More than just a campaign, Hoja en Blanco is a social movement that symbolizes trafficking survivors' potential to create a new future. Our goal with this movement is that the community would defend the victims' right to start over without being stigmatized.

Hoja en Blanco is also a call to fight for the liberty of those who are still in captivity. It is an invitation to people everywhere to join the cause, to change ideology and culture in order to write a new story both here in Mexico and throughout the world; one in which freedom, equality, and justice are the protagonists.

This campaign has spread to many nations and has united thousands of people, including government authorities, celebrities, and activists, both nationally and internationally. Among those fighting for liberty, Pope Francis stands out as an important figure. Two trafficking victims were able to meet with him during the World Mayors Summit in 2015. The campaign has continued to grow through concerts, plays, cultural events, forums, conferences, workshops...and now, this book.

*Blank Page* consists of ten true stories of trafficking survivors. They are genuine heroes, and their stories deserve to be heard. Some of the stories are narrated by the survivors themselves; others were written from personal interviews with them. After each story there are short informational sections based on research and personal experience (both mine and that of other activists) that support and illustrate central elements of the narratives.

At the end of this book, I will share a little more about how I came to recognize the huge need that exists and how I began—along with an incredible team of people—to help meet that need. I will also explain some of the strategies we are using to support the survivors and eradicate human trafficking.

You are about to read the stories of ten survivors who were trafficked for sexual or labor purposes and who, after years of support and accompaniment, are successful, established, and safe. In this book, they share their painful experiences in hopes that they can prevent other young people, full of life and dreams, from falling into the hands of traffickers.

This task is unending, and the work is not over yet. Here in Mexico, only six states have a specialized shelter for trafficking victims: Mexico City, the State of Mexico, Baja California, Puebla, Colima, and Chiapas. We would love to see the other twenty-six states in Mexico—and nations around the world—create private-sector refuges in cooperation with (and under the ongoing supervision of) the government.

Finally, I would like to emphasize that we don't have all the answers. For example, there is still so much we don't know in Mexico about boys and men who have been trafficked. We don't have shelters for victims living on the streets or for those who have contracted chronic illnesses, such as HIV-AIDS, as a result of exploitation. Just like any process, ours is the result of countless changes, of ups and downs along the path, and of continual learning.

What is certain, however, is that this book provides a solid basis to reflect on the problem of human trafficking. And in these pages, there are flashes of light that can brighten the dark night of slavery we are traversing. I share them because I know there are many who want to see this reality change. This is an invitation to you, the reader, to join us in the fight against human trafficking.

Our story begins with a promise: a promise of liberty. Together we can make a difference.

*To view a Spanish-language video that introduces some of the survivors whose stories are told in this book, scan this QR code with your smartphone camera or app.*

We regularly organize prevention campaigns in universities like the UAEM in Toluca. Special thanks to the dean, **Dr. Alfredo Barrera Baca.**

Performing artist **Yuri,** a great ally, has often supported victims, including playing Mixi in the theater production, *Del Cielo al Infierno* (From Heaven to Hell); as well as encouraging Luis Armando to file charges when she heard about his abuse.

**Ernesto Verastegui,** actor and producer of the movie *Little Boy,* 2015, and *The Sound of Freedom,* 2020.

**Raul di Blasio,** one of the greatest pianists in the world, has supported the Blank Page campaign, because all survivors have the right to compose their own new melody.

Professional soccer player **Darwin Quintero** and his wife **Valentina** have supported trafficking victims.

**Madaí** with **Luigi Ferrajoli,** Italian jurist who is considered one of the best civil liberties theorists in the world.

Concert in Ciudad Juarez, Chihuahua, with **Marcos Witt**, Christian singer, composer, and movie producer, who stands with the Blank Page social movement.

**Zunduri** with **Bill de Blasio,** mayor of New York, in the World Mayors Summit at the Vatican.

**Karla Jacinto** assisted in the training of more than twenty thousand police officers in Mexico City by telling her story.

# I. Lucero: Companionship

***The first time*** Lucero tried to commit suicide, she chose asphyxiation. She wanted to hang herself from the ceiling, but she didn't have the proper supplies to carry out her plan. If she would have had a rope, her story would have ended there. One day in 2015, a local newspaper would have run a small article about an Latina girl, identify unknown, without immigration papers, whose body had been found in an impoverished neighborhood of Washington, DC.

Lucero squeezed her hands like pliers around her neck, trying to cut off the flow of oxygen to her brain. She didn't know that it is impossible to commit suicide this way. The body has a self-protection mechanism that causes itself to faint when there is not enough oxygen; and, once unconscious, the body naturally begins breathing again. She discovered this for herself the moment she fell and hit the floor, panting, frustrated with her hurried plan and her inner demons: depression, insomnia, shame. And the constant sensation that her captor would come back for her—the captor who held her hostage for three years and forced her to have sexual relations with clients up to sixty times a day, seven days a week.

Months later, Lucero tried again. This time she chose pills. She took a fistful of the medicine she had been prescribed for stress and swallowed them. Lucero didn't know that the number of pills she ingested wasn't lethal: it was just enough to put her to sleep for a few hours. When she woke up, her torment returned, along with the frustration of not being able to kill herself.

Why did Lucero try to take her life twice, if she had already been through the worst: surviving three years of captivity, far from her own country, at the mercy of a captor who had ensnared her when she was still a minor?

Why was life so difficult for her *after* she had managed to escape her abuser? Why would Lucero, supported by a non-governmental organization, feel even more like dying now that she was free than when she was enslaved to the desires of "clients"?

"Because nobody was with me," expressed Lucero from someplace in the United States. "Because I was alone. You don't know the demons that talk to you when you are hurt and alone, or what someone is capable of doing when they feel abandoned."

A mortal loneliness.

\* \* \*

Lucero's story starts in a small point on the map of the western coast of Oaxaca, in one of those small towns forgotten by most of Mexico, until some misfortune strikes it. In a small park, on an afternoon like any other, a young girl, only thirteen years old, is approached by a sixteen-year-old boy. The world keeps spinning; nobody notices as these two teenagers become more than just strangers. They chat, they laugh, they exchange numbers, they set a date to meet again.

She doesn't know that he is a hunter of humans. He may be young for a tracker, but he's an expert. He spends his days walking through parks just like this one, in towns just like this one, looking for girls just like her, vulnerable at first glance. He gets them to fall in love with him using the strategy his family taught him: little compliments that turn into affection, affection that becomes promises, promises that end up in kidnapping for sexual exploitation.

He follows this pattern with Lucero. He speaks to her sweetly; they fall in love and become boyfriend and girlfriend. To show her his love is serious, he asks her to come meet his family, and together they travel to another small, unknown village in Mexico—unknown, that is, until a few years ago, when it became infamously known by the nickname "the birthplace of pimps": Tenancingo, Tlaxacala.

In Tenancingo, Lucero learns that her boyfriend's insistence to meet her own family was so that he could threaten to kill them if she didn't obey him. As soon as she arrives at the house of her boyfriend's mother, she witnesses with horror as the sheep's clothing falls off and he bares wolf's fangs. He informs her that her new home has become her dungeon, that she will never return to her family, and that she must accept her new fate as a hostage. Lucero spends hours locked up while he paces from room to room, making phone calls. Everything is uncertain until she is told that, finally, they will be leaving: a van is waiting, and a long trip awaits.

The car, traveling north, devours hundreds of kilometers. They reach the desert of Sonora where a *coyote*, a smuggler, is waiting. Their third attempt to evade Border Patrol is successful, and they cross by land, heading toward Tucson, Arizona. A long journey is still ahead: a journey that ends in Washington, DC.

In Washington, Lucero learns what her new job will be: having sex, time after time, in hotels, in rented flats, in rooftop rooms, in the back of vans. The clients are primarily immigrants, and she is required to satisfy them seven days a week, eighteen hours a day. The pay she receives is food, clothing, and the assurance that, if she gives all the money she makes to her captor and says nothing about her kidnapping, her family will not be murdered.

The night she is raped for the first time, dozens of clients turn her into the most recent victim of a well-known route for forced prostitution. It is a path documented by *The Discovery Channel* in the program, "From Tenancingo to New York," the second most-watched episode in Spanish and the winner of an Emmy. A painful gash of some 2,500 miles, every mile like stitches under the skin.

\* \* \*

From that day on, Lucero's life stops. It is like the torment of Sisyphus: a man who, punished by the Greek gods, was doomed to push a large stone up a mountain for all of eternity; but each time he approached the summit, the rock would roll back down to the bottom of the mountain. For Lucero, her punishment is pushing her life up a mountain of daily sexual abuse; and every morning, before dawn, she has to start all over again. It is like perpetually repeating the worst day of your life.

The daily sexual relations are as diverse as the clients: some are indifferent, others are sad, nearly all are violent. Even those who pretend to be affectionate mistreat her. Over the next three years, Lucero sees her body become covered with scars from Mexican, Honduran, Salvadoran, and American clients. But there is one that stands out in her story: an Indian with the soul of an anti-hero who puts a gun to her head and warns her that this life of prostitution isn't for girls like her. He says that the next time he finds her with men who are looking for sex, he will put a bullet between her eyes.

Lucero doesn't want to end up in a cemetery, but she doesn't want to go back on the streets, either. That night, she begs her dealer, her old lover, to let her go, because a client is threatening her life.

He refuses. "Just be careful not to run into him again," he replies, "but you can't stop bringing me my money." And that is how Lucero reaches her limit. After nearly a thousand days in captivity, she makes a bold decision. She steals the keys to the apartment where she is being held, carefully opens the door, and escapes.

A night shadow moves nimbly through the dark streets of Washington. It is Lucero, fleeing, choosing to live.

\* \* \*

The story could have ended there as well: "Young immigrant is detained for running, terrified, through the streets—a suspicious activity in a poor neighborhood—and, unable to prove her legal status, is deported." Or her story might have carried the simple headline, "Caught without papers!"

But the life of Lucero is also sprinkled with luck, even though it might not seem that way. During one of her trips to a client's house, she had noticed a place that appeared to be a hideout or shelter, and she took note, in case she ever decided to escape. This place becomes her first refuge before going to the police. There, she learns that there are organizations dedicated to helping women who have been victims of sexual exploitation, and she makes an appointment.

That is how Lucero finds an organization, in the capital of the United States, that helps survivors of domestic violence and forced prostitution. She is excited by the reception she receives, the promise of recovery, and, more than anything, companionship. What nobody tells her is that the NGO provides only temporary shelter for women, just like most civil and governmental organizations. After a year of living at the shelter with twenty-four-hour security, with her process of emotional recovery cut short, Lucero must leave the shelter, in accordance with the organization's policy. They need the space for more Luceros.

The most this organization is able to do is help her find an apartment where she can live on her own, although without the network of support and companionship that made her feel protected. The demons that had left her return to fill the empty places in her schedule. And even though she asks to return to the shelter to be with other girls like her, she is told no. There is no room. There is no bed for her.

"I couldn't handle my memories. I kept thinking they were after me, trying to kill me. I couldn't sleep. I began to eat too much and gain weight. I thought, *I can't do this anymore; I'm too tired; I have nobody to live for*," Lucero remembers. "I felt completely alone."

Besides the emotional pain, Lucero is tormented by a deep physical pain that stems from a particular night when she gave her trafficker less money than the daily quota he required. He hit her in the face so hard that he dislocated her jaw. Every night, she struggles to fall asleep, feeling as if her teeth are drilling into her gums. Only when exhaustion wins out is she able to get any sleep.

"I felt abandoned, as if I only mattered when I was first rescued, but not anymore. You can't accompany a survivor until *you* want to stop; it must be until *we* are ready. The problem is that they only take care of you for two or three months, maximum a year. After that, it's back to the streets. And a year is not enough to repair the damage done by all those people."

She continues, "I thought, *I no longer want to feel*, and I tried to choke myself with my hands. Then I took the pills. Would that have happened if I had someone accompanying me in the process? I don't think so. It was loneliness. They abandoned me."

\* \* \*

Her last recourse before a third attempt at suicide: Facebook.

Lucero remembers that once, during her captivity, she had seen a television documentary about a human trafficking survivor who was the honorary president of a Mexican non-profit organization named Fundación Reintegra (The Reintegration Foundation). The program stresses the importance of short, medium, and long-term accompaniment for survivors of human trafficking. It was being implemented by a foundation named Camino a Casa (The Road Home) and replicated by another group called Comisión Unidos vs. Trata (United Against Trafficking Commission). Lucero begins to see a ray of hope, and she decides to search for the organization on social media. She finds the page she is looking for. She writes, asking for help; and to her surprise, she receives a personalized response.

The companionship she was missing finally materializes. From Mexico, we coordinate the treatment plan Lucero needs so badly, one that would provide support until she is ready to be on her own. We build an alliance to help her: Tim Ballard, president of the Underground Railroad, plays a key role in getting her out of that lonely apartment and placing her with a family in the northern U.S. where she is welcomed as part of their home.

Now Lucero has a house. She receives psychological support. She receives the necessary dental work to repair her dislocated jaw. She discovers a community that helps her feel brave and valued. And ever since, the voices of the demons that haunted her grow further away, weaker, and more ridiculous.

"Everything is different now. I'm recovering without having to be hurried, at my own pace. I want to study. I want to become a writer. I also want to follow the example of Karla Jacinto and speak and be an activist fighting against human trafficking."

Another ingredient influenced the recovery of Lucero: the trafficker who had "fallen in love with her" is now in prison in the US. The Washington

19

police found him and caught him with the same determination he had shown against his victims. Today, the hunted hunter awaits his fate in a cold cell, not yet knowing how many decades he will spend in captivity for the crime of trafficking humans. And Lucero's testimony is key in sending him to a dungeon of his own.

For the first time since she was thirteen years old, Lucero is the owner of her time. She is living a life that is truly life, not punishment. She, and only she, will determine when her recovery process is over.

Perhaps one day in the next few years there will be a book on display in a store about an unknown, undocumented Latina girl who, with the help of many people, went from sex trafficking victim in a poor neighborhood in Washington to a survivor, a dreamer, and an activist.

The author of that book will be Lucero, and her face will smile from the cover; the girl who wanted to die has chosen to live.

# International trafficking, mental needs, and suicide

Human trafficking has always been a crime that spans borders and ignores cultural and language barriers. Its goal is to exploit human beings for profit. It is a business. In fact, it is one of the most lucrative illegal businesses in the world (the second-most or third-most lucrative, depending on which sources you consult). Human trafficking has grown to the point that it produces around 150 billion dollars in profit every year; 99 billion of that is related specifically to sexual exploitation.[1] Human trafficking doesn't discriminate: it only has eyes for money, power, and the domination of others.

Family-run "businesses" that traffic women and children are relatively common in Mexico. In states like Tlaxcala and Puebla, they may even be interwoven with cultural and social spheres. These families know that the "real money" is found in the United States, and traffickers all aspire to take "their girls" to the land of great opportunity.[2]

Beginning in 2010, various families who were frequently identified in cities like New York began to be investigated. These families repeatedly stood out in the testimony of victims, and it caused US investigators to wonder why all the traffickers came from specific states in Mexico. Something, they realized, must be behind that. The Granados family[3] was one of the first Mexican families to be identified for their role in organized crime and international trafficking. This family recruited young women using techniques based on romantic attachments and promises of a better life, full of dreams that quickly became fantasies in their minds, then just as quickly turned into the worst nightmares imaginable. Through threats, blows, and violence, they subjected their victims to prostitution with the goal of illegally crossing the border into the United States. There, separated from their families, from their culture, from their own language, it was much easier to keep them enslaved, especially with the additional threat of prison for being in a foreign country illegally.

And so began an alliance between the American and Mexican authorities, both sides working together to bring the reality of the trafficking of women between these two countries into the spotlight. This alliance has had very positive results. In 2017, another family with a similar trafficking history was caught: the Rendon Reyes[4]; and not long after, the Rojas Romero[5] family (who were linked to the Granados) was also successfully extradited. The work is never over. Identifying and investigating these cases is complicated, and it requires close cooperation between both countries.

The victims of these crimes are always uprooted from their normal life and from the security that comes from friends and family. Separating them from their home environment is one of the most crucial tactics in the process of enslavement. The instability and insecurity this creates causes the victims to submit more easily to the demands of the traffickers.

The overwhelming feeling of loneliness and isolation, combined with the high levels of violence by the trafficker and being raped by "clients" more than twenty times per day, all contribute to physical, social, and psychological consequences that are clear, yet very difficult to treat, once a victim is rescued.

Recently, more specific studies have identified links between suicide rates and human trafficking, especially when the victims are minors or young adults. The newest studies indicate that 23% of all trafficking victims attempt suicide at least once, while 53% have suicidal thoughts. This is significantly higher than the average rate for the general population, which is 3%.[6] This result is congruent with other mental issues and disorders evident in trafficking victims. In a study done in Asia among minors who had been exploited sexually, 56% suffered severe depression, 1 in 3 victims had signs of anxiety, and 1 in 4 suffered from post-traumatic stress disorder.[7]

Additionally, in March 2013, the French study, "Access to Health Care and Access to the Rights of People in Conditions of Prostitution that Comply with the Social and Medical Structures," carried out by FNARS and The French Institute of Public Health (InVS), showed that people working in prostitution are particularly exposed to physical and psychological violence, which has a significant impact on mental health and wellbeing.[8]

With respect to people working in prostitution, this study revealed that:

- They are 3 times more likely to have poor or very poor health compared to the general public.
- They are 7 times more likely to have suicidal thoughts than the general public.
- They take 4.5 times more anti-depressants and anti-anxiety medication than the general public.
- Nearly a third of those working in prostitution have considered suicide at least once in the last 12 months.
- The rate of suicide among the prostitution community is 12 times higher than that of the general public.
- Those in prostitution consume 4.5 times more sleeping pills than the general population (31% and 7% respectively).

These numbers should make us ask ourselves: how has it been so widely accepted as fact that trafficking victims can recover from their scars in a period as short as three to twelve months? Our experience has consistently shown us that positive results can only be achieved through long-term support and accompaniment designed on an individualized basis for each victim. Even though innumerable studies have demonstrated this to be true, the high costs, along with the commitment level required by those who provide these services, mean that reality often doesn't match the need. The government is certainly not able to sustain a task of this magnitude, which is why involvement by social organizations in the civil arena provides a fundamental, indispensable contribution. The care and recovery process of a trafficking victim is not possible without coordinated teamwork between government, society, community, businesses, educational institutions, and the services of physical and mental health professionals. Without the commitment and dedication of these important players, the survival of those who are or have been victims of trafficking becomes nearly impossible.

## References cited

1. E. Massimino, "Human Trafficking by the Numbers," 2016, http://www.humanrightsfirst.org/resource/human-trafficking-numbers (Accessed 28-June-2019).
2. "Entrevista con tratante 'Alex' en el reclusorio," Video property of Fundación Unidos vs. Trata, Mexico City, 2016.
3. Erica Pearson, "Guilty Plea from Thug in Mexico-to-NYC Sex Trafficking Ring," New York Daily News, 2-Mar-2012, https://www.nydailynews.com/new-york/guilty-plea-thug-mexico-to-n-y-sex-trafficking-ring-article-1.1032305 (Accessed 4-Aug-2019).

4. Department of Justice, office of Public Affairs, "Eight Members of Mexican Sex Trafficking Enterprise Plead Guilty to Racketeering, Sex Trafficking, and Related Crimes," 12-Apr-2017, https://www.justice.gov/opa/pr/eight-members-mexican-sex-trafficking-enterprise-plead-guilty-racketeering-sex-trafficking (Accessed 4-Aug-2019).

5. U.S. Immigration and Customs Enforcement, "4 Mexican nationals extradited to US for international sex trafficking offenses," 5-Apr-2018, https://www.ice.gov/news/releases/4-mexican-nationals-extradited-us-international-sex-trafficking-offenses (Accessed 12-Sep-2019).

6. L. Frey, J. Middleton, N. Gattis, and A. Fulginity, "Suicidal Ideation and Behaviour Among Youth Victims of Sex Trafficking," US National Library of Medicine, Crisis Journal, Issue 40 (2019), 40-248, 30-Oct-2018.

7. Kissil, Yunk, Pocock, and Zimerman, "Exploitation, violence, and suicide: Risk among child and adolescent survivors of Human Trafficking in the greater Mekong subregión," US National Library of Medicine, JAMA Pediatrics Journal, Volume 169 (2015), 8-Sep-2015.

8. ProSanté, "Acceso al cuidado de la salud y el acceso a los derechos de las personas en situación de prostitución que cumplen con las estructuras sociales y médicas," Santé Publique France - Institut de veille sanitaire, 146 (2013), https://www.santepubliquefrance.fr/maladies-et-traumatismes/infections-sexuellement-transmissibles/vih-sida/documents/article/etude-prosante-2010-2011-sur-l-etat-de-sante-l-acces-aux-soins-et-l-acces-aux-droits-des-personnes-en-situation-de-prostitution-rencontrees-dans-d (Accessed 10-July-2019).

# II. Mixi: Gratitude

*When I think* of my childhood, I remember happily climbing up and down mountains of trash. As soon as I got home, I would run toward those foul-smelling piles of garbage that were my neighbors, climb them gleefully, and slide back down. Over and over again I would scale them, feeling invincible; thinking that this was not just a playground, but a training ground for life. If I could climb up the hills of waste and become stronger, nobody could hurt me. But I was wrong.

My house was a speck of poverty erased from the maps in a marginalized community of Cuautitlan, Izcalli, a dusty municipality in the metropolitan area of Mexico City. I grew up between a mine and a landfill, next to my aunts and uncles, my younger sister, my grandmother, and my mother, who was so young everyone thought she was my sister.

The day I made my debut into this world as a daughter, and she as a mother, she was only fifteen years old. I remember that instead of taking care of me, she used to go out and explore Mexico City, because we had just moved there from the country. She would give me a bottle to drink and, not caring that it might slip from my grasp, leave me locked in the house. The neighbors would hear me cry and call my father to let him know his baby hadn't eaten in hours. Every time he returned to the house, my mother would receive a beating. I think that's why she started to hate me.

Near the mine was a small lake. When I was three years old, I walked by myself to the edge. I would have drowned that day if my father hadn't arrived just as I was stepping into the water. He picked me up, furious, and marched into our home to demand my mother answer for her carelessness. Any other mother would have been frightened, would have hugged me, or, at least, would have shown some regret. But not her. She became upset and yelled at him to leave her alone; that I was her daughter, and she could do whatever she wanted with me. Even if that meant letting me die in a pit filled with water.

We lived in a house we shared with my uncle, who was maybe five years older than me. He was about fourteen years old, and I was eight or nine. My mother let him sleep with me, and he would take advantage of the sheets that covered us to touch me. One day my mom left me alone for several hours with him because she had errands to run. She came home early, unexpectedly, only to find me naked and her brother's hands on my body. She kicked him out of the house. But she never said anything else about the incident. She never taught me that what he was doing was wrong, that no one should touch me like that.

Eventually, my mom moved in with another man who became the father of my younger sister. In the dump, we made a house using four sticks and a tarp, like something you would set up for a party. Life there was anything but fun, though: we used boards, broken furniture, boxes, and sheets of aluminum as makeshift walls. When it rained, everything became very muddy. The grass was over a meter high, taller than me, and grasshoppers would jump everywhere, making me yell in fear.

I remember my stepfather with love. He was good to me because he didn't let my mother hit me. He won my affection by protecting me, but my mother soon ended the relationship with him. It seems my defenders were always temporary.

My mother held many different jobs. First she was a hair stylist, then she sold bread, and then she became a *fichera*, an escort, at a local dive bar, where she would drink or dance with customers to get them to buy more drinks. That is how she met her new partner: in the bar. His name was Mario and he was a waiter. My mother was a young girl, hungry for love, just like me. Soon after, she became pregnant and we moved to Tultitlan, also in the State of Mexico.

That was when the suffering for my family began, because Mario had problems with alcohol. My mother, because she was working at a bar, developed the same addiction. They would come home drunk every night and fight. Then she'd take it out on me. One time, shortly after we had moved, she was so drunk she couldn't get the apartment door open, so she threw the keys at me to open it. But she had never shown me which key to use. When I couldn't open the door, she grabbed me by the hair and started slamming my head against the door. I fell to the ground and she started kicking me. That day I stopped suspecting my mother hated me. I knew it for a fact.

I slept outside that night, leaning against the door, while she slept off her drunkenness in the comfort of her bed. In moments like those, I thought about what she had told me many times before: if she could have aborted me, she would have, because I ruined her life and her childhood.

Her life didn't last long. When I was twelve years old, she became ill. A virus developed in her medulla that consumed her: this woman, once explosive as a volcano, was reduced to an immobile shell in a wheelchair. The doctors said it was transverse myelitis, but nobody could explain how it entered her body. I think her hatred poisoned her. She stopped walking, and that started her descent to the grave: a catheter, a urinary infection, two failed kidneys, and so much alcohol running through her veins that hemodialysis couldn't keep up. A month later, on a Sunday, my mom ceased to be.

It was the middle of the night when Mario woke me up with the news. "Your mother is dead," he said matter-of-factly. I stood up and went to the doorway, but I didn't dare go in. I was afraid to accept that I was now alone.

My brothers, my stepfather, and I returned to my grandmother's house. Back to the garbage dump. I turned thirteen at the end of that month, and Mario was oddly loving toward me on my birthday. "You look just like your mother," he told me in a repulsive tone that made me feel dirty and afraid. The fact that I was growing up made me feel like I was dangerously close to ending up like her.

My story was one loss after another: a tale of temporary homes, each colder and more terrible than the last. I lived with an aunt, then with another, and then, finally, in a sewer with several other street kids. Even for me, a girl used to living among garbage, the sewer was too much. I had to get out of there, so I started wracking my brain, wondering where I could go. I remembered Elizet, the stepdaughter of my sister's father. She had introduced herself to me after my mom fell ill and told me that if I ever needed anything I could ask her for help. Her smile gave me confidence.

It's amazing what a small girl can do when she's desperate. I don't remember how, but I found Elizet. She and her husband happily welcomed me into their home. They were a young couple, in their twenties, with five children. Their love dazzled me when they told me how he had spent some time in prison for robbery and she never left his side.

Elizet received me as if she were my new older sister. She promised that things would be better for me and that I would go back to school. But she never fulfilled her promise. Soon, Elizet and her husband began to treat me very badly. They forced me to do all the chores in the house. Their children added to the abuse. The oldest, eleven years old, would spill milk on the floor on purpose and then order me to get on my knees and clean it up.

They lived luxuriously, or at least it seemed that way to me, a girl who grew up in a garbage dump. I remember their house in the State of Mexico as though it were a mansion. They also had a house in Cuernavaca and a hacienda in Queretaro. They kept their car collection at the Cuernavaca home. I would visit these places as their nanny, but I wasn't allowed to play; I could only watch their kids have fun.

Every day I would wake up at five in the morning and work until one in the morning, when Elizet would arrive, ask for a coffee, and order me to give her a foot massage. When I reminded her of her promise to sign me up for school, her answer was always the same. "If you go to school, I won't need you here. You want to go to school? There's a beauty school across the street." I didn't want to go, but she signed me up anyway so that, besides being her slave, I could cut and style her hair and take care of her nails.

Then Dulce came. The first thing I thought when I saw her is that she was just like me. She had also lost her mother. She was Elizet's neighbor, and when Elizet learned that her mother had died, she invited the girl to live in her house. From then on, she prostituted Dulce. She lied to her, saying she was saving all the money from the forced sexual relations so that Dulce could go to college. It never happened. Since Dulce had nowhere else to go, she resigned herself to her situation.

It was Dulce who told me that Elizet was a pimp and a prostitute. When my supposed older sister found out I knew her secret, she called me to her room and told me everything. "I make a living from prostitution. Now that you know, I want you to help me answer the phone."

That is how I turned into Elizet's double, using false names and faking accents of countries I didn't even know existed. My work consisted of explaining "the services": how long they lasted, what hotel to meet at, and the extra charges for lingerie or certain positions.

Six months passed, and I took care of the house and the phone calls. Until, one day, Dulce disappeared. I want to believe she escaped. Since they had lost the income they received from her, Elizet and her husband decided I would be a good substitute. To accomplish that, they added one lie to another. They said my sister's dad was dying and that his wish before becoming ill was that my sister would come live with Elizet. They said, "Your sister's father could still be saved, if you work with us and we buy him medicine. But if not, her father will die, and your sister will come live here. And you know what that will mean for her." They used fear to their favor, and I couldn't say no.

The first time was horrible. Elizet advertised threesomes in the newspaper so that we would both go in at the same time, and I would learn by watching her. Her husband stood outside the door in case I tried to escape. After two weeks of going to the hotels—after thirty, forty, sixty clients—the days lost meaning. I lived on inertia. My full routine in the house continued, but now I also spent my nights accompanying Elizet. The only time I ever slept was in transit, ten or fifteen minutes at a time.

I stopped crying. I also stopped laughing or dreaming. I even began hallucinating. I made up fantasies during the day while cleaning the house. I was a princess, an astronaut, a policewoman who fought against crime. These stories in my head began the weekend they locked me in a small room under the staircase while they went away on vacation. There was nothing for me to eat and I couldn't even go to the bathroom. The room had one little window covered with metal bars.

I slept for two entire days. When I woke up it was already Sunday. I heard them come home, but they didn't seem to remember I was there. I became desperate. I panicked. I began beating the door and screaming. I broke the glass on the window and tried to escape, but my body wouldn't fit through, and I ended up cutting my arms and my legs. With my own blood, I started drawing on the wall: a country field in the spring. It was full of wildflowers, and a knight appeared, dressed in black armor, who promised me one day I would be free. He encouraged me to not give up. When I dreamed, I traveled with him on his white horse. We would go to a glass castle that floated above Elizet's house. It was my dream refuge, my imaginary shelter. I was the only one who could see it and visit it. I had my own room, and there was a banquet awaiting me. Everything was perfect there.

One day, my sister called me. I immediately asked her if her dad was still on the brink of death. She was silent. "Are you still there?" I asked her after several seconds had passed.

"Yes," she replied, "but what are you talking about? My father is very well." I started crying again. My tears had returned. And so had my rage. I realized Elizet had lied to me.

I was more determined than ever to escape, but I was afraid. So I waited for the rage to return to give me energy. It happened a few days later: a man tried to force me to have sex with him without a condom and I said no. He hit me so hard that, for the first time, I dared to ask for help from an employee, one of the male housekeepers, who saw the scratches and scars on my skin and hid me in an empty room. When Elizet and her husband gave up their search, Ivan, the housekeeper, called a taxi for me. He gave me his sweater, I took off my high heels, and as soon as I saw the taxi parked outside, I ran to it and climbed inside.

We drove around the city for a while because Ivan was convinced we were being followed. When dawn broke, we went to his parents' house, and they lent me clothes and shoes. His family showed me a depth of kindness I had never experienced nor could ever repay.

The next morning, we bounced from one shelter to another. None of them accepted me. Some of the shelters required a payment to get in. Others only accepted children, and since I was already sixteen, I was too old for them. I was about to give up when we found a shelter that would take me as long as I first pressed formal charges with the Mexico City authorities. It was the first time I realized that what Elizet and her husband had done to me was a crime. I knew they had hurt me and they had lied to me, but Elizet had always told me that prostitution was normal, like selling furniture.

After my statement, the police put together a plan to detain Elizet and her husband by calling one of the phone numbers to solicit a service. A police officer would pretend to be a client and then make the arrest. But when they called, all the phone numbers had been disconnected. So they arrested Elizet and her husband in their own house on December 10, ten days after I escaped.

I arrived at Fundación Camino a Casa on December 2. My dream became reality: I wanted a home, a roof, a family; and I found them. Germán and Lorena Villar, activists who worked at the foundation, went to pick me up at the police station. After everything I had gone through, they both expected to find a broken young girl, but they didn't: I was happy, even ecstatic.

When I saw the house where I was going to live,

I fell in love. There was little furniture and no curtains. It was a house that had been abandoned for a long time, but it was my home. When I walked in, I became the princess of my castle.

That night, after dinner, Germán and Lorena talked with me in private. "This is Fundación Camino a Casa. We are here for you. You are not alone," they told me.

"But I don't have anybody," I interrupted them, because I still believed what Elizet had told me for so long.

"That's not true. From this moment on, you have us," answered Germán.

I still remember those words.

I soon started calling him Dad. In his loving company, my heart could finally rest. We spent a lot of time together, strengthening my spirit. With the certainty that somebody loved me, I was able to finish elementary school, middle school, and high school, and then I began working toward a career in communications at the Iberoamerican University. I also joined Fundación Reintegra.

One day, Germán died. A tragedy. The worse of them all. I began to feel alone and depressed again. Sadness overcame me and I dropped out of college. Later, thanks to the support of Fundación Reintegra (which, after Germán's passing, was overseen by some Americans), I went back to college to study finance.

I'm still working on that. I'm good at school. I've learned that I am intelligent and dedicated. My dream is to work in the stock market and learn how to invest, to make money grow, and to be able to finance many projects. I want to work at the National Bank of Mexico for a few years to gain experience, then start my own financial coaching business for organizations, helping small and medium businesses. I would also love to be the mom I never had but know I am capable of being.

But, above all, I want to be an example so that more and more girls can see that it is possible to escape situations like mine and dream again. We just need someone to dream with us. Someone who can tell us that the world is not a garbage dump, but a beautiful glass castle.

*To watch a Spanish-language video of Mixi's story narrated by her, scan this QR code with your smartphone camera or app.*

# Child trafficking

Human trafficking is hidden in plain sight. When we were working on the proposal for the General Trafficking Law of 2012 here in Mexico, we realized we needed to carefully study the different ways that this crime affects our communities.

From a legal perspective in Mexico, the "General law to prevent, sanction, and eradicate human trafficking crimes and to protect and assist the victims of these crimes" recognizes eleven different types of exploitation. These include servitude or slavery, sexual exploitation (such as pornography and forced marriages), labor exploitation, forced labor or services, forced begging, forced adoption of minors, using minor for criminal activities, organ trafficking, and the use of human tissue in illegal biomedical testing.[1]

From an international perspective, despite the controversies and nuances which may arise in different countries regarding classifications, and taking into account that different governments must contextualize and adjust the prosecution of crime according to the paradigms of each culture,[2] the Palermo Protocol is the main international treaty that functions as a foundational judicial reference for human trafficking laws. This treaty declares that, at the minimum, the definition of human trafficking should include exploiting the prostitution of others

Figure 2.1

# Human trafficking crimes according to Mexican law

I. Slavery

II. Servitude

III. Prostitution of others or other forms of sexual exploitation

IV. Labor exploitation

V. Forced labor or services

VI. Forced begging

VII. Using persons under eighteen years of age for criminal activity

VIII. Illegal adoption

IX. Forced marriage or arranged marriage for dowry without consent

X. Trafficking of organs, tissue, or cells of living persons

XI. Unlawful biomedical experimentation on persons

Source: Comisión Unidos vs. Trata

or other forms of sexual exploitation, forced labor and services, slavery or other analogous practices, servitude, or the extraction of organs.

Unfortunately, in Mexico, child labor exploitation and domestic servitude (which fall under the category of labor exploitation) continue to be a painful daily reality; and the statistics are not promising for child victims of trafficking. The National Human Rights Commission estimates that seventy thousand children are being sexually exploited in this country,[3] and the United Nations Office on Drugs and Crime, in its diagnosis of the trafficking situation in Mexico, estimates that at least twenty-one thousand minors will be ensnared by trafficking networks each year.[4]

Regarding non-sexual labor exploitation, the results of the Childhood Labor Module of the National Census Bureau's 2017 report, reveal that the number of boys and girls working in Mexico is 2.5 million; 2.2 million of those are working illegally.[5] Along with this study, and based on the most recent National Survey of Work and Labor, 658,000 minors work in Mexico's agricultural fields. Of those, 66% work in family fields and are not included in the above statistics; however, 223,741 boys and girls are being forced to work illegally just in agriculture.[6]

Mexico's National System for Integral Family Development commissioned a report titled "A study of child and adolescent laborers in 100 cities," one of the most complete studies to date on minor workers in urban zones. This study counted 114,497 child and adolescent laborers between the ages of 0-17 in the urban areas of the country, approximately 9,000 of whom live on the street.[7] Of these minors who are working in cities, the above-mentioned Labor Module documents that 42.5%—almost half—do not receive any income, and that 28.8%—more than one fourth—earn just one minimum salary (less than $7 US) in exchange for an entire workday.

In addition, the National Counsel for the Prevention of Discrimination (CONAPRED, from its initials in Spanish) conducted a study titled "Household Workers" in which they concluded that 36% of domestic workers began working as minors, with an average education level of sixth grade, and that 21% of the girls started before they were even fifteen years old, which is illegal in Mexico.[8]

These numbers are devastating, and if we take them at face value, we must admit that more than 1.4 million children in this country are experiencing some form of human trafficking.

There are many ways to trap someone into being trafficked, but they almost always include hope-inducing promises, especially in the case of young girls who have suffered serious lack in some area. Working as a *fichera*, a bar girl or escort, is one of the most common, well-disguised tricks to pull young girls into the commercial sex industry. The victims are typically very young women who are offered a temptingly high wage in exchange for encouraging men to drink more alcohol in night clubs, cabarets, or strip clubs. They are required to dress provocatively to entertain the men while they consume as many drinks as possible; all paid for by the man, of course. Within a few hours, the girl is under the influence of alcohol herself and is subjected to all manner of assault and abuse. Many of the establishments of this type in border towns, such as Tijuana, have hotels on the upper floors where the women are expected to prostitute themselves to create more income for the club.

The work is full of subtle manipulation and deceptive promises, with the goal of ensnaring the women in sexual exploitation and addiction. It is one of those jobs to which women consent without fully understanding what they are getting into. Even though they receive income, the high fees they must pay usually cause them to be exploited, and very soon they become addicted to alcohol and often other drugs. Invariably, the only people who actually end up making money are the owners of the clubs. The reality is that if girls want to earn money as *ficheras*, they must be willing to get drunk and to be groped, pinched, slapped, licked, spit on, and subjected to all manner of abuse; and to have sexual relations with violent, drunk clients.

This is a form of human trafficking through sexual exploitation, but the women rarely identify themselves as victims because the majority of them consented to take this "job." The General Law against Human Trafficking of 2012 protects women in this situation by stating that consent does not disqualify an activity from being criminal.

That is the case of Mixi. Her story is a tale of multiple kinds of exploitation, wrapped up in a beautiful life. Seeing it through her eyes is something that can't be ignored. Just as her life was rescued, others can be rescued as well.

## References cited

1. Diario Oficial de la Federación, "Ley general para prevenir, sancionar y erradicar los delitos en materia de trata de personas y para la protección y asistencia a las víctimas de estos delitos," 14-June-2012, http://www. diputados.gob.mx/LeyesBiblio/ref/lgpsedmtp.htm (Accessed 12-sep-2019).
2. United Nations, "Protocol to Prevent, Suppress, and Punish Trafficking in Persons, especially Women and Children," December 2008. https://treaties.un.org/pages/ viewdetails.aspx?src=ind&mtdsg_no=xviii-12-a&chapter=18&lang=en (Accessed 12-Sep-2019).
3. Comisión Nacional de Derechos Humanos, "Diagnóstico sobre la situación de la trata de personas en México, CNDH, México, Distrito Federal," 2013, http://200.33.14.34:1033/archivos/pdfs/ diagnosticoTrataPersonas.pdf (Accessed 12-Sep-2019).

4. Oficina de las Naciones Unidas Contra la Droga y el Delito UNODC, "Diagnóstico nacional sobre la situación de la trata de personas en México, Oficina de Enlace y Partenariado de UNODC en México," 2014. https://www.unodc.org/documents/ mexicoandcentralamerica/ Diagnostico_trata_de_ personas.pdf (Accessed 12-Sep-2019).
5. Instituto Nacional de Estadística Geografía e Informática INEGI, Módulo de Trabajo Infantil (MTI) 2015, Indicadores Básicos y Tabulados, http://cuentame. inegi.org.mx/poblacion/ninos.aspx?tema=P (Accessed 12-Sep-2019).
6. Secretaría de Desarrollo Social, Encuesta Nacional de Jornaleros 2009, Módulo de consulta de resultados, http://www.cipet.gob.mx/Jornaleros/.
7. UNICEF, DIF Nacional. "Estudio de 100 ciudades," 2003, México. http://www.laisumedu.org/DESIN_Ibarra/ salon/si2/ti-06.pdf.
8. Consejo Nacional para Prevenir la Discriminación, CONAPRED, "Trabajadoras del Hogar Ficha temática," 2017, https://www.conapred.org.mx/userfiles/files/ Ficha%20TH(1).pdf.

# III. Neli: Education

*If you listen*, can you hear Neli crying?

She breaks down when she talks about the house where she grew up. Her voice cracks when describing the one-room shack with wooden walls and a palm-branch roof where she lived. The house had no door, and to keep wild animals from getting in at night, they had to block the entrance with a barrel. Hundreds of nights were spent sleeping while tangled in the terror of an attack from a wild animal. Years later, she'd have the same fear, but of a different type of animal. You will read more about this fear, but for now, what you need to know is that to speak of this house is, at the same time, to speak of poverty and of violence. Of a deep pain that, although now overcome, still moves the soul.

That is why Neli cries.

\* \* \*

I grew up in Tres Valles, Veracruz, close to the border of Oaxaca. A region of the world where you can feel the heat strike you as powerfully as the poverty. On my street, similar to every other street in the area, there was no electricity, no clean water, and no restrooms. My father was a farmer who cut sugar cane and planted corn in the fields in front of our house. As you might expect, we never had enough money.

To get to school, I had to walk thirty minutes under the burning sun or in the never-ending rain. Upon arriving at the bus stop, another thirty minutes would be spent riding the bus before we arrived at school. There, I was always discriminated against for my dark skin and lack of money. Nobody was rich, but I was the poorest of the poor. I remember wearing worn-out shoes and old clothes, something the other children made sure to point out every morning.

My father's friend worked on a lush ranch that seemed to sprout money. Every weekend, when the fruit to feed the cattle arrived at the ranch, my father's friend would set some apart for us without his bosses' knowledge, because he knew we couldn't afford to eat well. It was only on those days that we were able to enjoy one of the few luxuries we knew: eating fruit meant for animals.

\*\*\*

Before continuing with the story, it is important for you to know that Neli's father was an alcoholic. Maybe that appears to be a small detail compared to the other tragedies of this story, but that seemingly inoffensive fact will turn out to be a deciding factor for her future. He was also violent. On more than one occasion, Neli witnessed him beat her mother. She remembers one time in particular when he threw a five-liter milk jug at her head, a blow that could have killed her, and he didn't even seem to care.

Nevertheless, Neli thinks of him with gratitude. Despite the poverty in which they lived, he insisted she go to school. He made sure to wake her up every morning at four o'clock to attend elementary school. Later, he enrolled her at the "best" public middle school in the region. Unlike the other schools that only offered classes on Saturday, this one went from Monday to Friday. And after middle school, he supported her through high school.

Just a month before Neli was supposed to graduate, her father passed away. For her, the death of her father was the event that marked the beginning of her story as a trafficking victim. The loss of her father, the fragmentation of her family, the abandonment by other relatives, and her loneliness led her to believe the promises of love of a trafficker, someone who filled the paternal void her father left behind.

\* \* \* \*

My father died when I was eighteen years old, one month before I graduated high school. "You have to study, because that's the best inheritance I can give you," he told me. That's the reason I worked hard and left my town. I began to study tourism in a town nearby that had a college. To support myself, I worked in a shoe store, but they paid me very little. I survived on coffee and bread.

I ask you to imagine my father's death like an explosion that catapulted me far outside my bubble of protection. Or like a blast that launched me into the worst years of my life, because my mother and brother went to live with my maternal grandparents, and I chose to live with my aunt. Months later, because I wanted to live closer to the university, I began to rent an apartment with a friend from school. One Saturday, during my lunch break at a job I had found, I went to a park to eat. A man approached me and introduced himself as Alex Guzmán Herrera, twenty-five years old, originally from Queretaro. He told me he had lived in New York, where he spent some time working in construction, and now he lived in Puebla. When I had to return to work, he asked me for my phone number, and I gave it to him. He called me the same day.

He was a gentleman, charming, an experienced flirter. He sent me messages every day, and after two weeks he asked me to be his girlfriend. I didn't agree because we had only known each other a short time; but he kept insisting, until finally he convinced me. I accepted on the condition that he ask my aunt's permission, so one weekend, we went to my aunt's house, who was the sister of my father. She welcomed him and gave her approval because he seemed like a responsible person and because he said he made his living renting out seven apartments he owned, and his plan was to buy even more. You would have liked him too; he seemed like quite the catch.

After that, he and I would chat alone, outside of my aunt's house. One day he brought up the idea of marriage, because I was very mature and he needed a wife. I said no because my priority at the time was to finish college. I got tired of his stubbornness and decided to end the relationship.

But he was an expert hunter. He knew exactly how and when to attack again. We got back together soon. He would visit me and we would go out to eat, like normal couples do. I tried to break up with him again, because I was feeling overwhelmed by my studies and my job. When I told him, he hurt me with that sharp tongue of his: he said that's fine, to keep my classes, but they would never bring me love or happiness.

A few days later, he again carried out that effective rhythm of absence and return. We had one last date in Córdoba, Veracruz. He was near tears as he pleaded with me. "Baby, you're so pretty, and I love you so much. I am going to have to go back to New York and find an older woman because the girls my age don't take me seriously," I remember him saying. I thought he was sincere, and I cried with him. He made one last attempt. He said if I would, right then, agree to move to Puebla and live with him, I wouldn't lack for anything, including my education and economic support for my family. In the back of my mind, I knew it was crazy to say yes because I'd only known him for two months. It wasn't sensible... but I also knew that I had started to love him. I agreed.

I'm sure it's hard for you to understand. It's even hard for me to understand what I did. But there's no way to go back now. We walked to his car, and he handed me a letter telling me I was the love and the light of his life. The letter would have made you fall in love, too. It was full of places we knew and sentimental phrases that were cliché but effective. We set off on the highway from Córdoba to Puebla, talking the whole way about everything we wanted to achieve together.

By the time we got to Puebla it was evening. We ate at a mall called Plaza Dorada, where he bought me a pair of white sandals. A Cuban musical group was playing in the mall, and he sang the verses of the song sweetly in my ear. At the end of the day, he took me to a storage building which he claimed belonged to his boss, a supposed architect, and we made ourselves at home.

I spent the entire next day cleaning the storage area, which was in reality just a dirty room. I found women's underwear, blouses, pants, money hidden in envelopes, cell phone cards, voter ID cards, and a letter from a man to his son. When I asked Alex about all these things, he calmly told me that for years he had helped people cross the border into the US and that the immigrants left behind things they couldn't take with them. It sounded believable, reasonable.

You should know that Alex was very good to

me. He would buy me gifts, we would eat at restaurants, and we would walk around downtown Puebla and Cholula together. He opened up a whole new world to me. After two weeks of being there with him, he started asking me strange questions. He asked me if I would ever leave him under any circumstances; to which I always responded that I would never leave because he was my husband and I loved him very much.

Sometimes he would bring up his friend's wife who made money as a "sex worker," and he would say that if I wanted to do the same, she could teach me. It scared me when he talked that way, so I would change the subject, and everything would become pleasant again. But one day, he came home drunk and began to insult me. He told me I wasn't worth anything as a woman and that, if I really loved him, I'd start working to help him. He swore to me that he had a financial problem and needed money, or the men to whom he owed money would kill him. I was silent, and I tricked myself into believing his mistreatment of me was due to the alcohol.

A few days later, at a restaurant, he gave me an ultimatum. He told me that if I wouldn't start working as a prostitute, he would leave me, because if a woman really loved her husband, she'd give her life for his. The only way we could stay together is if I agreed he could offer my body to strangers. He knew I had a poor relationship with my family, so he would manipulate me by telling me that if I left him, the only thing I'd have would be a house where nobody loved me.

I don't expect you to understand me, but I tell you all this so that maybe you can put yourself in my shoes. I felt as though I had no option but to stay by his side. I accepted his offer with a broken heart and a mind drowning in fear. Alex had met my mother and brother at a family gathering on the anniversary of my father's death, and he had even visited the house where I grew up. That is why I didn't dare escape, because he knew where to find my family and he could hurt them.

A few days after he threatened me, he took me to the Puebla bus station to meet Lucero, who supposedly was the wife of his friend. Alex didn't travel with me to Mexico City; he sent me with her. On the bus, Lucero explained to me what the work entailed and how much I should charge, although Alex had already explained everything to me. They both told me to pick a new identity, my "artist" name. I chose to call myself Nayeli.

We arrived at Mexico City's western bus terminal and got on the subway. I suppose that under other circumstances I would have been amazed by an underground train, but my mind was somewhere else. I barely remember getting off the subway at the La Merced stop, in the heart of the prostitution corridor of downtown Mexico City. First, we went to the Hotel Necaxa, where we showered and got ready for the night. Then, Lucero took me to Hotel Las Cruces, but no one believed I was nineteen, so they turned me away, thinking I was a minor. So Lucero worked out a deal with another woman, and between the two of them, they found a spot for me in the Santo Tomás alley. Carolina told me everything: how much to charge for the "room service," where to stand, how to answer each question, and how to make money in the shortest amount of time.

When I went into the room with my first client, tears rolled down my cheeks. I couldn't believe it. I felt every assault rob me of my dignity. I cried again with the second client. After that, I got myself under control and chose to be strong to avoid getting reprimanded.

La Merced was a horrible place. The clients were of all types and backgrounds, including students and foreigners. Some of them were filthy, others violent. There were about fifty women, including myself, in the alley, and I would say ninety percent looked like victims, whether because they were so young or because I could hear how they spoke to their pimps. They looked so sad. I saw how some of the victims later became the victimizers; teaching and guarding the new girls.

When I began menstruating, I asked the alley pimps for a break, but they denied my request. I mention that detail to whoever reads my story so you can realize the abuse they made us endure. Instead of a break, the traffickers would give us a sponge with alcohol on it to place in our vaginas; supposedly, this would stop the bleeding. That's when I realized that breaks were a privilege only for people with freedom, and I wasn't free.

In the alley, we would walk in a circle so the men could see us and decide which woman they wanted. We would check the clients to make sure they weren't carrying guns or knives and that their cell phones were turned off. We were charged for the condoms that were given out for free at the IMSS, Mexico's public hospital system. Every evening, the pimps would pour a smelly liquid on the street which, according to them, attracted customers.

Our services lasted a maximum of ten minutes in small rooms that had curtains instead of doors. Inside was a concrete slab with a thin mattress covering it, and a mirror on the wall. It was a misery similar to my childhood. Remember when I told you I slept in fear because the room had no door and I was afraid of wild animals?

In this case, the animals were called clients.

\*\*\*

On July 24, 2010, Mexico City law enforcement carried out a raid in our area, La Merced. It was one of the first raids in the city. Everything happened so fast. One moment, you are in a tiny room being raped, just like every other day; and the next moment you are out in the street, watching police officers and government officials swarm the Santo Tomas alley. All of us women were brought before a public court to testify so that the authorities could determine which of us were victims and which were traffickers. When they questioned me, I didn't tell the truth. I was a faithful soldier for my trafficker. I said I was in La Merced because I wanted to be there, that nobody was making me do this, that I didn't know anybody else, that I liked being there, that I had to support my family and save money to go to college. I recited the Alex taught me to say if there were ever a raid.

Those who questioned me didn't believe what I said, and they thought I might even be a minor, so they decided to send me to Fundación Camino a Casa.

I still remember the moment vividly and with deep emotion: the door of the shelter opened, and behind it was a girl who would later become my best friend. She didn't know me, but she embraced me, and she told me my hell had frozen over, and my physical and mental safety would never again depend on a man who rented out my body.

Believe me: everything changed in that moment. With a door. The door I never had as a child.

\* \* \*

Understanding Neli's story is the key to understanding a strategic point used among human trafficking rings. Like her, many victims don't admit to being victims when they are first rescued. The majority have been trained to deny they are being exploited, and some repeat the exact words dictated to them by their traffickers out of fear that the traffickers will carry out their death threats against the victims and their families. Many of the victims aren't even aware human trafficking is a criminal offense; they don't believe that what they are going through is a crime or a form of violence.

Other victims are deceived in the depths of their hearts, and they try to protect their traffickers at all costs. Neli believed she was in love. She thought her actions were acts of love toward a man who needed her help. When the authorities revealed to Neli that Alex had deceived her using a fake name, and she wasn't the only one, but he had exploited other young woman as well, Neli realized that, from its very beginning, what she thought was a story of love was actually a story of crime.

It is a crime that ensnares 341,000 people in Mexico, according to the Walk Free Foundation. One that exists throughout Mexico, but to a greater extent in twenty-one states. One that is controlled by forty-seven criminal organizations, ranging from entire families to drug cartels. A crime that depends on suffering to exist.

If we held a minute of silence for every victim, this country would spend 236 days in silence.

\* \* \*

After two weeks in the Fundación Camino a Casa shelter, a police commander came to speak with me. "You do have a pimp. Lucero works for him," he told me in a tone of iron conviction. I was surprised, because supposedly Lucero was the wife of Alex's friend, whom I never met. That's when I realized that Alex didn't love me, that he was only interested in the money I gave him. A righteous rage took root within me, and I agreed to press charges and cooperate fully with the authorities in order to arrest him. That is when I told the truth.

The police and I set a trap on Circunvalación, the wide street that connects the alleyways of La Merced. There, I was to meet with Carolina and ask for Alex's address, claiming I needed to take him some money. But Carolina never came; instead, a woman named Mary did. She approached me with a cell phone and a phone call for me: "Go to Puebla right now. When you buy your ticket, use a different name." It was Carolina's voice on the line.

The agents who were with me arrested Mary and took her to the local station to make a statement. It turned out she was another one of Alex's victims. With her help, we set up a second trap, and Mary led the police to the house in Puebla where Alex was living like a king from our suffering. His cellphone contained the most convincing proof: there were hundreds of photos of minors and girls like me, listed in catalogs as if they were objects, and an enormous number of incriminating messages. One of them I remember well: Alex, my husband the trafficker, repeating the same words of flattery he had used on me, but now on a fourteen-year-old girl, his next victim.

Later, I learned the true name of Alex Guzmán

Herrera was Arturo Galindo Martínez. He wasn't twenty-five years old, but thirty-four. He wasn't from Queretaro, but from San Pablo del Monte, Tlaxcala, a town that births as many traffickers as there is grass on the side of the road.

Initially, in April 2016, both Arturo Galindo Martínez and Lucero were sentenced to thirteen years, nine months in prison. Eventually Lucero came to be considered a victim as well, so in March 2019 she was released, and her remaining sentence was added to that of Arturo, giving him twenty-seven years, six months in prison.

\* \* \*

More than eight years have gone by since Neli was rescued. Various organizations have played a role in her process of reintegration, included Fundación Camino a Casa, Reintegra, and Unidos vs. Trata. She is a part of the first generation of survivors who were cared for using a long-term model, financed by a Mexican civil association and focused on finishing her education.

For three years she worked in a business incubator called Emprendium, led by the businessman René Villar. While there, she found an interest in gastronomy. She remembered the lack of resources in her hometown in Veracruz, and she thought food could be a way of escape for people there. A restaurant could benefit from her neighbors' abilities, boosting employment and income. Human trafficking, she thought, could be eradicated by over-coming poverty.

In the summer of 2016, Neli obtained her bachelor's degree in business administration, with honors, from La Salle University. What she learned in the classroom, along with her work experience (Neli has worked in other startup environments, including travel agencies and telecommunication companies) allowed her to open her first restaurant in Mexico City in early 2017, in partnership with an old friend from her hometown and with the support of programs from the Secretary of Labor.

\* \* \*

In order to heal, Neli has had to think about how to tell her own story. When she tells it, even though it costs her a few tears, she is reconciled with her past; she owns her present; and she exercises her freedom to keep anyone else from determining her destiny.

Currently, Neli is studying her master's in business administration at a prestigious university. She also devotes time each week to her YouTube Channel, "Cocina con Neli" (Cooking with Neli), where she shares weekly recipes from her beloved Veracruz. And if being an entrepreneur wasn't enough, Neli is also an activist. With the help of @SinTrata, an organization by young people for young people whose mission is to help prevent human trafficking, she visited the Universidad Tecnológica del Centro de Veracruz (Technological University of Down-town Veracruz). Using her testimony, she warned people about the way criminals in that region oper-ate. Her hope is that this information will make a difference in the short term by keeping the number of victims from growing. Meanwhile, she continues to study English, thanks to a scholarship from the ex-ambassador of Britain, Duncan Taylor; and she continues each day to strive toward reaching her long-term dreams.

Neli gets excited talking about the new restau-rant she will be opening soon. This one will have a beautiful door, something she never had as a child, and through that door hundreds of diners will en-ter and congratulate her for her work.

To speak of this restaurant is to speak of strength, of survival, of love for others, of a pro-found happiness that moves the soul.

If you listen, you can hear Neli crying...from happiness.

*To watch a video about Neli's journey, scan this QR code with your smartphone camera or app.*

# Hidden vulnerability

One of the fundamental aspects to learn and understand when working with trafficking victims is that their stories rarely start the moment they are exploited. In every case, there is a backstory, usually one of vulnerability: a state of being that goes hand in hand with the tragedy of being deceived, used, sold, and destroyed.

Mexico, unfortunately, is a country with the ideal ingredients to provide the crime of human trafficking with new victims. The *Global Slavery Index*, published by Walk Free Foundation in 2018,[1] states that 57% of Mexico's population is vulnerable to human trafficking. The diagnosis of this crime in Mexico published by the United Nations Office on Drugs and Crime in 2014 shows that poverty, low levels of education, lack of opportunities, discrimination, and marginalization are common indicators of the country's vulnerability. The most worrisome part of this evaluation is that women, girls, and boys are the social groups at the greatest risk.

With respect to poverty in Mexico, the most recent numbers from the Consejo Nacional de Evaluación de Política de Desarrollo Social, or CONEVAL (National Counsel for the Evaluation of Social Development), show that 42% of the population lives in these conditions. Approximately 7.4% of

Mexicans currently survive in situations of extreme poverty. For those under the age of 18, the probability of belonging to this group increase to 51.1%, and for woman in rural areas, it increases to 85.1%.[3]

This is directly correlated to the lack of available jobs for high school graduates, and this, in turn, is related to the high level of school dropouts, as well as the lack of access in some areas to free, quality education. The study "Panorama de la educación 2017" (Education Panoroma 2017), conducted by the Organization for Cooperation and Economic Development (OCDE, from its initials in Spanish), reports that 53% of the Mexican population between the ages of 25 and 34 do not have a high school diploma and only 17% have any level of college education.[4]

The lack of opportunity is apparent in a study conducted by the Instituto Mexico de la Juventud (Mexican Youth Institute), which states that of those who do graduate from university or technical school, only 30.7% acquire a job.[5] In the case of indigenous and disabled populations, discrimination and marginalization are even more intense. The National Council to Prevent Discrimination (CONAPRED, from its initials in Spanish), places the number of people from indigenous ethnic groups who report being victims of discrimination at 40.3%. In the case of people with a disability, the percentage increases to 71.9%.[6] These two facts make clear how vulnerable these populations are to criminal networks dedicated to such crimes as human trafficking.

Sadly, according to "The National Diagnosis on the Situation of Human Trafficking in Mexico," the highest risk factor for vulnerability is simply being a woman: 70% of the victims of human trafficking around the world are women and girls.[7] In 60% of these cases, the purpose was to exploit them sexually. An analysis of trafficking done by Comisión Unidos vs. Trata A.C. shows that 21% of victims are enslaved or sold by their own families.

Human traffickers are professionals in identifying vulnerabilities, deficiencies, and the deepest desires of their prey. They have been trained to ask key questions in order to learn the victims' deepest desires in order to later take advantage of them.

Oscar Montiel, in his thesis, "Human trafficking: pimps, initiation, and modus operandi," highlights the practices and customs adopted by the families of certain municipalities in Tlaxcala who have made their living as pimps and traffickers from generation to generation. Montiel discovered the most popular *modus operandi* is getting the victim to fall in love. Traffickers are experts in manipulation and psychological analysis. They are capable of quickly identifying how to get into a victim's life: by taking advantage of the weakest aspect of the prey; that is, the most obvious need of the person they are trying to seduce. From a young age, the traffickers are training in this subtle art: the art of the tongue. Once a potential victim has been found, all the efforts of the victimizer are focused on the conversation, on connecting with whatever emotion has been missing. This situation—which is trivialized when it is accepted as a way for the families and the state of Tlaxcala to improve their economy—continues to be an extremely profitable business due to the huge and nonstop demand created by "clients" who are always willing and ready to pay.[8]

As a society, it is easier to believe that they—the women who have been deceived—are the ones who consented to leave with their traffickers of their own free will. This is due to not understanding the innate desire in all human beings for improvement, for working toward something better, for not remaining stuck, but for the opposite: growing, seizing opportunities, and living a better life. Traffickers are aware of this inherent desire within every human being and take full advantage of it. Therefore, we need to have a greater awareness of it ourselves. It is important to mention that, although the indicators show a greater vulnerability in certain social groups than in others, no one is exempt from being deceived and manipulated by one of these experts.

# References cited

1. Walk Free Foundation, Global Slavery Index, 2018, https://www.globalslaveryindex.org/2018/data/country-data/mexico/ (Accessed 12-Sep-2019).

2. Oficina de las Naciones Unidas Contra la Droga y el Delito, "Diagnóstico Nacional sobre la situación de trata de personas en México," México: Secretaría de Gobernación, 2014, https://www.unodc.org/documents/mexicoandcentralamerica/Diagnostico_trata_de_personas.pdf (Accessed 4-Sep-2019).

3. Consejo Nacional de Evaluación de Política de Desarrollo Social, CONEVAL, "Medición de pobreza 2008-2018 de los Estados Unidos Mexicanos," 2018, https://www.coneval.org.mx/Medicion/PublishingImages/Pobreza_2018/Serie_2008-2018.jpg (Accessed 4-Sep-2019).

4. Instituto Mexicano de la Competitividad IMCO, "Panorama de la Educación 2017 vía OCDE," 2017, https://imco.org.mx/educacion/panorama-la-educacion-2017-via-ocde/ (Accessed 12-Sep-2019).

5. Instituto Mexicano de la Juventud (IMJUVE), Dirección de Investigación y Estudios sobre Juventud: Diagnóstico de la situación de los jóvenes en México," August 2013, https://www.imjuventud.gob.mx/imgs/uploads/Diagnostico_Sobre_Jovenes_En_Mexico.pdf (Accessed 12-Sep-2019).

6. Instituto Nacional de Estadística Geografía e Informática INEGI, "Una de cada 5 personas de 18 años y más declaró haber sido discriminada en el último año: Encuesta Nacional sobre Discriminación (ENADIS) 2017," Press release #346/18 (2018), 1-3, https://www.inegi.org.mx/contenidos/saladeprensa/boletines/2018/EstSociodemo/ENADIS2017_08.pdf.

7.  Oficina de las Naciones Unidas Contra la Droga y el Delito, "Niños y niñas, casi un tercio de las víctimas de la trata de personas: informe de UNODC," 2016, https://www.unodc.org/colombia/es/press/2016/diciembre/informe-global-trata-de-personas.html (Accessed 12-Sep-2019).

8.  Oscar Montiel (2009), "Trata de personas: padrotes, iniciación y modus operandi," Inmujeres, Ciudad de Mexico, http://cedoc.inmujeres.gob.mx/documentos_download/101080.pdf (Accessed 12-Sep-2019). Cited in the doctoral thesis by Rita Maria Mellado Prince Contreras, "Políticas públicas para desalentar la demanda de explotación sexual," 2018.

# IV. Zunduri: Freedom

**She appeared on** the front page of national and international newspapers. It was the top story on radio and television. On Twitter, the hashtag #Zunduri was trending the afternoon of April 28, 2015, and for more than three hours, the hashtag was one of the most posted in the country, right up with the president of Mexico and the international boxing star Manny Pacquiao. Thousands of people, some for the first time, openly discussed the phenomenon of modern-day slavery in Mexico, picking up pieces of information from the alphabet soup of words chosen by journalists and editors to tell her story.

The story that everyone read and listened to was told in the words of others, but now this story will be told in the first person. These are the words of Zunduri, as she has never spoken them before.

\*\*\*

At the end of my story, there will be a happy ending. I promise. I will travel to places I had only seen on television; I will hear my name spoken by the most powerful people in the world; and I will speak about human trafficking in forums around the world.

I will be at a beautiful restaurant, as the sun is setting, with my face lit up by a flickering birthday candle, placed by people I love, on a cake so beautiful I hardly dare touch it. On the other side of the windows, I will see stretched out before my eyes Buenos Aires, Argentina, and streets that seem to come straight from of a painting. With me will be my second mother, Rosi Orozco, and countless allies who treat me like a movie star as we celebrate my first year of freedom. With the sound of a tango warming my heart and the night protecting me under a blanket of constellations, I will be convinced that life is wonderful.

But that is the future. There are many years of suffering before that unforgettable day arrives. I need to tell you my story from the beginning, because there is no other way to do it: I will start at the lowest point to finish at the highest.

\* \* \*

I grew up in Mexico City in a violent family that consisted of my mother, my older sister, and me. My sister and I are daughters of different fathers, and my mother always pointed out our differences: my sister was the beautiful one, the obedient one, the one who deserved everything. And I was all the antonyms.

When I was eight years old, my mother sent me to live with my godmother. She wanted me as far away from her as I could be. It hardly seemed possible, but life became even harder. My godmother always complained about me. "You are useless" was a phrase I heard day and night. Years later, she also threw me out of her house, and I ended up at my paternal grandmother's house. She eventually rejected me as well, and I was sent to my father's house. And from there, I was sent to a boarding school where I finished elementary school with great difficulty.

Next I went to another boarding school, this time in Cuernavaca, where I experienced a tumultuous start to middle school: some of the girls were very violent and they would hit, steal, and even sexually abuse the other girls. The staff at the boarding school was overwhelmed; there were too many girls, so keeping oneself safe was a solitary task. It was there I realized there would never be a loving place for me.

I remember calling my mom one day and begging her to take me out of the school because I couldn't handle it any longer. To my surprise, she did. I went back to live with her. I enrolled at the middle school partway through the year, but being the "new girl" made me a target of bullying by my classmates. My fragile self-esteem couldn't take it and I started skipping school.

"You aren't going to be treated like a princess around here," my mother told me one day when I had skipped classes and been found out. "You have to get a job." And that is when my story takes a very dark turn.

* * *

Soon I ended up with an aunt in Ramos Arizpe, Coahuila. I continued my middle school education there at a *secundaria abierta*, a Saturdays-only school, while at the same time working at my aunt's restaurant as a waitress. When I turned sixteen, I returned to Mexico City. The deadline for high school admission exams had passed, so once again, I looked for a job.

Around that time, I reencountered Leticia, someone who would be key to my story. She was the mother of an old classmate from elementary school, Jannet. I barely recognized her when she came into the bakery I was working at. She looked at me carefully, sharply, and recognized me as well. She wrote her phone number down on a piece of paper and invited me to go to her house. I did, and soon I began to trust her.

It must have been her maternal appearance that made me tell her how my relationship with my mother had gone from bad to worse. And that I had a boyfriend, Miguel, whom I had moved in with at seventeen years old, hoping to flee violence, but who beat me nearly every day.

When I expressed to her how alone I felt in the world, Leticia offered me a roof and shelter. "I will love you like a mother, and I will give you everything you are missing. What more could you want?" she asked me. She was right: that was all I ever wanted.

\* \* \*

"Human trafficking: crime that exploits the most vulnerable," was the title of Amnesty International's global campaign in 2018.[1]

"Women and children, the most vulnerable to human trafficking," declared the headline of a blog from Mexico's Presidency in July 2018.[2]

"57% of Mexicans are vulnerable to human trafficking," said a publication by Walk Free Foundation.[3]

\* \* \*

When Leticia and her husband came to pick me up, it was a cold night. I had just fought with Miguel, and it was clear things couldn't continue as they were; so I had called them, and they arrived like my saviors.

The breakup with Miguel, although it was the right thing to do, hurt me so deeply that I fell into depression. I cried all the time, asking myself over and over again, *Why didn't things work for us?* I stopped caring about my job at the bakery, and I skipped work so many times that they fired me.

Leticia could not take this. She said I couldn't just spend my days doing nothing, that I had to contribute to the household. "I understand you completely. I know he broke your heart, but we need you to at least pay for the food you eat," she told me. "You have to help with the household chores."

At first, the chores were simple. Then they began to pile up. Months later, when the fifteenth birthday of Leticia's daughter was coming up, she needed help at the family's dry-cleaning business. When she put me in charge of the business, I felt very responsible and important.

There was another girl working at the dry cleaners. Her name was Yadira. Without intending to, a rivalry started between the two of us. I felt as though she hated me because Leticia had put me in charge and it was my job to make sure she did her work well and on time. At the same time, Leticia demanded there be no complaints from the customers. But I was still depressed, and the sadness distracted me all the time. Yadira took advantage of this and began to steal money and sabotage my work. Soon, the sales and receipts didn't balance, and the clients' orders had mistakes.

One morning, facing a customer's fury over a burnt sleeve, Leticia had to pay for my mistake from her own pocket. She got angry and slapped me. I screamed that she had no right to hit me, and she responded with more punches and kicks. I remember she told me I had to iron extra hours to pay back the money from the burnt shirt, plus the money missing from the register. "It will be three dozen items a day," she ordered.

From that moment on, any time Leticia needed money, she would try to get it through me. Any excuse was enough to make my debt grow. I started by ironing three dozen clothing items, which had to be finished in four or five hours. If I didn't finish on time, she would add another dozen. If one shirt still had a wrinkle, she demanded another six. Three dozen items a day became five, then eight. Little by little, those eight became ten or fifteen.

My life went into spasms. It was filled with work, stress, and fear, because the punishment for mistakes wasn't just piles of clothes, but beatings. Eventually, I lost my right to leave the house. I didn't even have time to take a shower, so I smelled terrible. "You disgust me," Leticia told me one day. "You aren't going to sleep in this house with me or my daughters. Go to the dry-cleaning shop." There was no bed there, not even a blanket or a mat. I had no other option but to sleep on the floor. Without realizing it, my entire life was now dedicated to Leticia. I didn't have so much as a free moment to untangle my own hair. Three years went by.

\* \* \*

It was December. While I was ironing, I found some cash folded up in a shirt. I escaped to the corner store where I bought all the little things that I had missed in those three years: chips, cookies, gum, chocolate... When I returned, Jannet, my old classmate, was waiting for me. She immediately went up to the house to tell her mother. That is where the scar I still carry on my back was born: from the broomstick Leticia used to beat me.

"I found the money in a shirt!" I explained,

thinking the punishment would stop. Instead, Leticia picked up the hot iron and pressed it against my left arm. Time felt eternal as my skin burned. The pain was indescribable; the smell nauseating.

"This is so you learn that everything in this place is mine. You owe me more than that. If you find a bobby pin, fifty cents, whatever, you must give it to me to pay your debt," she said.

The punishment didn't end there: I had to iron two dozen more items. Between all the absurd punishments, the quota was now nineteen dozen items a day. I couldn't allow it to rise any higher. I tried to escape one day when neither Leticia nor her daughters were at home. I went outside and took a taxi to a friend's house, but the person who opened the door told me my friend no longer lived there because she had gotten married. At that moment I realized I'd been working as a slave for three years.

I got back into the taxi and poured out my story to the driver. I told him I had problems with the woman I was living with, that I didn't know what to do and had nowhere to go. He replied that the only way he could help me was by letting me live with his sister, who was a single mom and lived in the same neighborhood. So I did that.

I worked as a babysitter for a month, believing that Leticia had given me up for lost. I was relieved to not have to put up with her torment. I didn't know it at the time, but during the month I was hiding, she designed a plan to enslave me again. She offered Yadira, the other girl working at the dry-cleaning business, her liberty in exchange for testifying against me: in other words, she would forgive her "debt." That is how Leticia found a witness to testify against me in court on a charge of theft.

She looked for me. She hunted for me, with police assistance. And she found me, one day, walking through the streets of the neighborhood. "I've reported you to the police for theft!" Leticia screamed at me. "Imagine what your family will say, after years of not hearing from you, only to discover you're a thief."

Everything was perfectly coordinated. A patrol car pulled up behind her with an imposing police officer inside. "I want to be good to you," said Leticia. "What would you prefer? Jail or my house?"

Obviously I didn't want either option, but the officer who got out of his car assured me that, if I didn't agree to Leticia's terms, I'd be in jail that night. I was alone. Terrified. Ignorant of the law.

"Come back to my house and work for three months, and after that, your debt will be paid. You'll work Monday through Sunday, eight dozen items a day. You can eat and shower on your own time. If you don't bother me, I won't bother you," she assured me.

If three years had already flown by, what was another three months? I gave in.

\* \* \*

"The chilling story of Zunduri, the 'slave at the dry cleaners,'" ran the headline of the daily Mexican newspaper *Vanguardia*.[4]

"The painful story of the 'slave' from Tlalpan," announced a Mexican website run by *Publimetro*.[5]

"I thought it was normal for them to hit me, like a daughter being corrected," quoted the international newspaper *El Pais*.[6]

\* \* \*

During those three months, Leticia didn't beat me or yell at me, but she repeated day in and day out that I was alone, that I had nowhere to go, that the only person who would unconditionally support me was her. She always reminded me that my mother had never looked for me because I didn't matter to her. She even told me that she ran into my mother one time, but she told Leticia her life was better without me. Who needed blows when those words, all the time, were my torture?

Shortly before our agreed-upon term expired, Leticia gave me a pair of boots. There was a note attached: "I love you like a daughter. The best thing for you is to stay with me, because you won't be safe anywhere else." I believed her, so I let several more months go by, until I had lived with her for a full year. A year that evaporated in the steam of an iron and the smell of cheap starch.

I wanted to restart my life, but I had no one I could turn to, so I sat down with Leticia and told her my plans. I spoke from my heart, believing that if she saw my vulnerability she would see me for who I was: a girl who knew there was more beyond the dry-cleaning shop and who wanted to experience it. When I finished speaking, she threw herself at me and began beating me furiously, screaming that I was an ungrateful wretch. "Not even your life could ever repay everything I have done for you. Listen closely: not even your life. So don't come to me telling me you want to leave. If you ever leave this house, you will leave dead."

From that moment on, the physical abuse grew more intense, and the workdays became longer, unending. If I didn't finish the ironing on time, they would beat me, usually with a cane. There wasn't even time to eat. Between the beatings and the lack of food, my body became weaker and weaker.

Another year went by. In total, five had passed.

\* \* \*

Jannet became pregnant; but she still beat me until I bled. She would tear my fingernails, inflict wounds on my head, split my lips. If I dared to defend myself, Leticia would jump at me, calling me uncaring because Jannet's pregnancy was high-risk. Both of them would burn any part of my body that was still whole. They would hit me with whatever they found at hand: plumbing pipes, kitchen utensils, canes, electric cords, hangers, brooms, rocks.

The months during Jannet's pregnancy were hell. And then it got worse. A day before the baby shower, Leticia and her daughters cleaned up the house. They found that the wall and the ceiling of the living room were splattered with my blood. They painted over it, trying to hide the evidence of my torture.

The day of the event, early in the morning, Leticia woke up and ordered me to bathe. She didn't even give me a chance to take off my clothes before she began dumping buckets and buckets of cold water over me. When I complained, she began beating me with the cane. The blood mixed with the water. I didn't even know where I was bleeding from anymore. With her fingernails, Leticia ripped the scab off a deep wound on my head, which smelled terrible from the buildup of pus inside. She made me kneel, then she emptied a bottle of vinegar over all the wounds. "I hope you don't plan to complain about anything else. The people who are coming here today had better not even hear you breathe," she said.

When she left me alone in the bathroom, the first thing I did was look in the mirror. It had been a long time since I had seen myself in one. I didn't recognize myself. I was swollen, I was missing two teeth, and I had bruises everywhere. I was deformed.

I got dressed in five minutes and went down to the dry-cleaning shop, where Leticia had a surprise for me. She had purchased a chain. She wrapped the chain around my neck and threw me a haughty look. "This is how animals like you are treated. You brought this on yourself."

Throughout the day, she came and went between the baby shower and the dry-cleaning shop. I begged her to take off the chain because it was making my work impossible. She finally gave in so I would have no "excuses": she took it off of my neck and wrapped it around my waist. The baby shower ended, the guests left, but the chain remained.

From that moment on, I was a woman attached to a chain. I slept standing up. I would go days without eating, sometimes five in a row; in my hunger, I would even chew on the plastic we used to protect the clothes and eat body lotion. They decided when I could go to the bathroom; many times I wet myself, and they punished me with blows. Everything became a reason to beat me, to the point that the cane they used to strike me broke in two. They replaced it with a plumber's wrench and electrical pliers. During the last beating I remember, Leticia pressed a hot iron on my head, my neck, and my lips.

Had any more time passed, I would have been dead. But one day, after letting me go to the bathroom unchained, Leticia didn't secure the padlock all the way. She didn't notice, but I did. For three days I pretended to be chained, all the while planning my escape. On the last night, like most other nights, she came down to supervise my work. I ate the few bites of food she offered me, and I slept for a while. Around five in the morning, I woke up. I put on a hat a customer had left behind, a scarf to cover my face, and a sweater. I pushed the ironing board up against the bathroom wall and climbed out of the window and onto the patio of the house. I ran as hard as I could. As hard as my legs would let me. As hard as I desired to be free.

In the shadows, I saw a taxi. This time, I promised myself I would never return.

\* \* \*

I gave the taxi driver my friend's address, the woman who had helped me with my first escape attempt, and he took me there. When I saw her and told her my story, she advised me to report the situation to the police. When dawn came, her son-in-law took me to various hospitals, but none of them would treat me unless I filed a police report first.

The next day, I filed a report with the department of justice in Mexico City. Three days later, a judge issued a warrant, and my abusers were arrested. I had to go identify the physical location of the criminal charges. When I entered, I felt sadness. Leticia had tried to erase the evidence of my torture from the walls, but there were still traces. Blood is not easily erased.

I immediately returned to the hospital. My physical recovery wasn't easy. The initial evaluation of the doctors was that my body was in the condition of an eighty-year-old woman. The official report of physical injury included more than six hundred scars.

Rosi Orozco came to meet me at the hospital. She helped get the doctors to care for me more quickly. After the exams, the doctors explained that the situation was complicated, but that I would heal. From that moment on, Rosi and I became inseparable.

I chose not to go to the shelter. After a childhood in boarding schools and five years locked up in Leticia's house, what I most desired was freedom. My recovery, now that I was free, was so quick that I surprised everyone. All I knew was that I wanted to make up for the time that had been stolen from me. I overcame slavery with an enormous desire to live. I wanted to devour the world in a single bite.

\* \* \*

"The laundromat slave: 'I want to eat the world in hours,'" headlined the Peruvian newspaper *El Comercio*.[7]

"Zunduri, a new life for the ex-slave who shook Mexico," wrote the Brazilian newspaper *O Globo*.[8]

"One year of freedom: the dry cleaners' slave laughs again," stated the international portal of *CNN in Spanish*.[9]

*＊*

Sometimes I can't believe how much my life has changed. I went from being locked up to flying across international borders. That trip to Argentina, Buenos Aires, and Córdoba as a representative of Fundación Camino a Casa was my first trip outside of Mexico, and since then I seem to have grown wings. After South America, I traveled to the Vatican where I shared my testimony with more than fifty mayors from around the world, and I visited Miami, Florida at the invitation of *Telemundo*. I became a voice, alongside Karla Jacinto, for the campaign *Hoja en Blanco* (Blank Page), which promotes new opportunities for human trafficking survivors.

I know some authorities have criticized me for traveling and sharing my experience, but I'm convinced that deep down, what really bothers them is when victims share a platform with politicians, scholars, or wealthy people. They want to make us feel that our voices are not as important. They don't respect the fact that a victim is a person, with the freedom to make choices.

That same year, my traffickers received their sentence: Leticia, Ivette, Jannet, and Jose de Jesús were each sentenced to thirty years in prison. While they sleep in a cold cell, I live in peace. I work as a conference speaker against human trafficking, and I share my testimony through the theater production *Alas Abiertas* (Open Wings) with another survivor, Karla de la Cuesta. I've received invaluable support from the civil association @SinTrata, led by Mariana Ruenes, as well as from a prominent businessman, Andrés Simg.

When people ask me about my life, I love answering that not even slavery could chain my dreams to hopelessness: I want to finish school, to own a bakery, and to build a family. I will teach my children that no human being should ever be treated like that. That freedom is the most important thing people can have. That love always finds its way through violence.

In particular, though, I love to tell them about that beautiful restaurant in Buenos Aires. About the tango music vibrating through my body as I discover that not even years of abuse could take away my desire to dance and feel alive. About the sensation of loving my life, while the city lights below remind me I'm in a country that is new to me. About the eternal gratefulness deep inside my chest that gives me peace to continue to follow my dreams: soon I will have a bakery, and I will bake beautiful cakes, like the one in front of me, for unforgettable moments such as this.

It is the happy ending I deserve.

\* \* \*

"Zunduri's captors locked away for 30 years," wrote the Mexican newspaper *Excelsior*.[10]

"From slave to student: Zunduri's new life," broadcast the Hispanic TV channel, *Televisa*.[11]

"Zunduri, the young woman who broke chains of slavery in Mexico," said the daily Panamanian paper *La Estrella*.[12]

And a headline that doesn't exist yet, one that waits and watches for Zunduri's future, in some national or international newspaper:

"Zunduri's slow-cooked freedom: human trafficking survivor now a successful baker."[13]

*To view a Spanish-language news report and video interview with Zunduri, scan this QR code with your smartphone camera or app.*

# Slavery among young people

The General Trafficking Law of 2012 defines slavery, in Article 11, as: "The dominion of one person over another, depriving that person of the unhindered control of their person or goods, and exercising toward the person the traits property ownership."[13]

Since then, two cases of slavery under the stipulations of Article 11 have been reported in Mexico. The story you just read is the closest to the law's definition of slavery, and it is a story the entire country and the world came to know.

An analysis of human trafficking around the world, and especially in Europe and the Americas, indicates that those at highest risk of falling into some form of exploitation are boys, girls, and teens living on the street; those who identify as LGBTQ; those who have lived within an institutionalized care system such as orphanages; and, more than any other, those who have run away from home due to physical or psychological abuse, abandonment, or sexual assault.[14]

It is highly alarming that, in Mexico, we do not have sufficient information regarding youth who have run away from home to escape abandonment, mistreatment, or abuse. The last survey was done in the late nineties, and it is not worth including because it is so outdated. However, we can get an idea of the probable state of the issue in Mexico from a 2013 study conducted by the Institute of Medicine and the National Research Council of the United States, which documented that 20% of young people living on the streets had been victims of human trafficking; 15% of those were exploited sexually, 7.4% were exploited in areas of labor, and 3% were a combination of both. However, when young people who identify themselves as LGBTQ are included in the metric, the percentage goes up to a horrifying 33.3% of victims. This means that one in three LGBTQ youth who live on the street has fallen victim to some form of human trafficking.[15]

More recent research that can serve as a reference was done in 2017 by Loyola University and Pennsylvania University; in their studies, researchers interviewed more than nine hundred young people who had run away from home. They found that 40.5% of the women, 25.3% of the men, and 56% of those who identified as LGBTQ had been exploited sexually; 91% had received fraudulent job offers as bait. Of those who were exploited for work, 81% participated in activities related to drug trafficking. A total of 95% of the trafficking victims had been abused at home and 49% had suffered sexual abuse.[16]

As long as we as a society are not willing and committed to doing a better job at reducing the number of young people who end up on the street, looking for what they could not find in their own homes, it will not be possible to reduce the number of human trafficking victims among our boys, girls, and teens. Our attention must not be diverted: our children are the future of our countries. What class of society are we, or will we be, if we don't take care of them today? And what hope would there be of achieving a more equitable society?

## References cited

1. Buada Blondel G., BLOG, "Trata de personas: Delito que explota a los más vulnerables," Amnistía Internacional, 2018, https://www.amnistia.org/ve/blog/2018/07/7220/trata-de-personas-delito-que-explota-a-los-mas-vulnerables.
2. Comisión Nacional para Prevenir y Erradicar la Violencia Contra las Mujeres CNPEVCM, "Día mundial contra la trata de personas," 2018, https://www.gob.mx/conavim/articulos/dia-mundial-contra-la-trata-de-personas-167781?idiom=es (Accessed 12-Sep-2019).
3. Walk Free Foundation Global Slavery Index, "Regional Analysis: Americas," 2018, https://www.globalslaveryindex.org/2018/findings/regional-analysis/americas/ (Accessed 12-Sep-2019).
4. *El Universal*, "La escalofriante historia de Zunduri, 'la esclava de la tintorería,'" 2-Dec-2016, https://vanguardia.com.mx/articulo/el-escalofriante-caso-de-zunduri-la-esclava-de-la-tintoreria.
5. *Publímetro*, "Las duras confesiones de la 'esclava' de Tlalpan," 28-Apr-2015, https://www.publimetro.com.mx/mx/noticias/2015/04/28/las-duras-confesiones-de-la-esclava-de-tlalpan.html.

6. Luis P. Beauregard, "Veía normal que me pegaran, era como un correctivo a una hija," *El País*, 30-Apr-2015, https://elpais.com/internacional/2015/04/30/ actualidad/1430420689_369540.html.

7. Redacción EC, "Esclavizada en lavandería: 'Quiero comerme el mundo en horas,'" *BBC Latinoamérica*, 19-May-2015, https://elcomercio.pe/mundo/latinoamerica/ esclavizada-lavanderia-quiero-comerme-mundo-horas-364477.

8. Redacción EC, "Zunduri, a nova vida da ex-escrava que comove o México," *BBC Brasil*, 26-Apr-2016, http:// g1.globo.com/mundo/noticia/2016/04/zunduri-a-nova-vida-da-ex-escrava-que-comove-o-mexico.html.

9. R. Romo, "Un año de libertad: la esclava de la tintorería vuelve a reír," *CNN*, 18-May-2016, https://cnnespanol. cnn.com/2016/05/18/un-ano-de-libertad-la-esclava-de-la-tintoreria-vuelve-a-reir/.

10. F. Cruz, "Sentencian a familia que esclavizó a joven en tintorería en Tlalpan." *Excelsior*, 2-Dec-2016, https:// www.excelsior.com.mx/comunidad/2016/12/02/1131742.

11. Noticieros Televisa, "De esclava a estudiante; la nueva vida de Zunduri Ana Laura," *Noticieros Televisa*, 29-May-2017, https://noticieros.televisa.com/historia/de-esclava-estudiante-nueva-vida-zunduri-ana-laura/.

12. Redacción digital *La Estrella*, "Zunduri, la joven que rompió las cadenas de la esclavitud en México," *La Estrella de Panamá*, 30-Apr-2015, http://laestrella.com. pa/internacional/america/zunduri-joven-rompio-cadenas-esclavitud-mexico/23862238.

13. Diario Oficial de la Federación, "Ley general para prevenir, sancionar y erradicar los delitos en materia de trata de personas y para la protección y asistencia a las víctimas de estos delitos," 14-Jun-2012, http://www. diputados.gob.mx/LeyesBiblio/ref/lgpsedmtp.htm (Accessed 12-Sep-2019).

14. Institute of Medicine (IOC) and National Research Council (NRC), "Sexual Exploitation & Sex Trafficking of Minors," 2013, https://youth.gov/youth-topics/trafficking-of-youth/sexual-exploitation-and-sex-trafficking (Accessed 12-Sep-2019).

15. Institute of Medicine (IOC) and National Research Council (NRC), "Confronting commercial sexual exploitation and sex trafficking of minors in the United States," Washington, DC: The National Academies Press, 2013:1, http://www.nationalacademies.org/hmd/Reports/2013/Confronting-Commercial-Sexual-Exploitation-and-Sex-Trafficking-of-Minors-in-the-United-States.aspx (Accessed 12-Sep-2019).

16. Covenant House, "Largest-ever research studies find one-fifth of surveyed homeless youth in the United States and Canada are victims of human trafficking," New York, NY, 2017, https://www.covenanthouse.org/charity-blog/blog-news/largest-ever-research-studies-find-one-fifth-surveyed-homeless-youth-united (Accessed 12-Sep-2019).

# V. Camila: Love

*It was just* a plastic bag. Black, opaque, a little bulky. Capped with a tight knot. Camila was given it while she was trying to think where she could work. She had a technical degree in tourism administration, so in her mind there was the possibility of being a receptionist in a hotel, much like the one she was living in. Being a waitress was another option, or perhaps a housekeeper, or a hotel maid—whatever she could do to help her distressed husband, who had just told her his brother had a huge debt with the bank and needed a loan urgently or he would go to prison.

"Don't worry about your brother," Camila had told Armando, trying to calm his false anxiety with a sweet caress. "I can help you. That's what we're here for: to support one another. You tell me what to do and I'll do it."

Sitting on the edge of the bed, Camila was going over the options open to her as a twenty-five-year-old girl, new to the capital city of Puebla. That's when her husband tossed the bag into her hands. It weighed next to nothing, its contents indiscernible from the outside.

"All I need is your ID," he said with a cavernous

tone she had never heard before. "I found you a job. That's your uniform."

Camila untied the knot. She opened the bag. At the bottom, she saw a red pleated skirt, like a schoolgirl's, but extremely short. Under that piece of fabric was other one, thin and lacy, barely enough to be a translucent blouse.

"You're going to work today. As a whore."

\* \* \*

At one time, Pie de la Cuesta was nothing but water. Located on the coast of the state of Guerrero, it was a lagoon where only fish and abundant tropical vegetation could be found. Mangroves sprouted like the foam on the waves and animals crawled across the sand, moving with the same natural rhythm as the palm trees that stretched into the sky and cast coconuts to the ground. It was a virgin paradise that was destined to become a top tourist destination in Mexico.

Halfway through the last century, this destiny became a reality several kilometers south, in the port town of Acapulco, with the inauguration of the Miguel Alemán Coastal Highway, a tourism-friendly drive which soon attracted luxury hotels, restaurants, clubs, and extravagant apartment complexes with beautiful views. The port city quickly became a favorite vacation destination for foreigners and nationals, due to the permissiveness of the authorities toward the visitors whose pocketfuls of cash kept the city alive.

The jet set of the world—artists, singers, politicians, movie stars—flocked to the sun and sand of Guerrero, but so did money launderers, drug dealers, pedophiles, and pimps. Customers who demanded drugs and sex with an ocean view came to Acapulco, and criminals came to the port, along with honest workers, from surrounding towns such as Pie de la Cuesta.

That is where Camila was born, in one of those neighborhoods where the dirt floor burns the feet of its inhabitants. The daughter of a violent mother and an explosive father, she grew up so unprotected that when her best friend raped her at sixteen years old, she knew she had been left alone in the world. Her parents falsified her documents, dressed her up as older than she was, and forced her to marry her abuser. The beatings she had received as a child followed her to her new home, and they didn't even cease when she became a mother.

Tired of the blows, Camila decided to flee Pie de la Cuesta. She wanted to try her luck in the port of Acapulco, where it was easier to find a job and start over. And, for a few months, her plan worked: she was studying toward a technical degree and working in a restaurant. Until luck went astray and led her to the Miguel Alemán strip, where she met Armando, who introduced himself as a lost tourist looking for "La Quebrada," the renowned spot where masculinity is demonstrated by throwing oneself headfirst off a cliff and into the sea.

Armando pretended to need a guide to take him through the port city, and Camila innocently offered to help. That day, as dusk settled, they walked the boardwalk together. The friendliness, good humor, and intelligence of the man immediately attracted Camila, and she gave him her cell phone number when they said their goodbyes. A few days later, messages from Armando started coming; then phone calls, sweet dates together, presents. And after eight months, a wedding proposal. At nine months, Armando traveled with his brothers to Pie de la Cuesta to formally ask Camila's family for her hand in marriage.

A month later, they both moved to Puebla to live closer to Armando's family. They started from nothing, as she had always wanted: a hotel room was the seedbed for the young couple's dreams.

The first three months were a honeymoon. It seemed like, finally, the beatings that had followed Camila since her childhood had stopped. They ate at restaurants, they went shopping, they fell asleep happy and woke up to kisses...until the day that Armando came home with a stunned face and exaggerated seriousness. He asked her to forgive him for his gloomy mood, but his brother, he said, had received an ultimatum: pay off his credit card debts or face court and eventually a jail cell.

"You have to help me. I've given you the life of a queen, and now I need you," begged Armando. And Camila, thankful, offered to do anything he asked of her. Anything.

As Camila mentally reviewed her employment options in this city she barely knew, Armando tossed the black plastic bag at her; he commanded his wife to try on clothes shorter than anyone would wear even at the height of an Acapulco summer.

"You're going to work today. As a whore." He snapped at her, his face as grim as a grave-digger.

"No! Of course not. Armando, are you joking? I'd rather die..." she responded.

"I'm not asking you. I'm telling you. You start right now."

Camila felt a stabbing pain. A vortex of sand and saltwater churning in her stomach. She wanted to throw the clothes back at him, scream, and hit him. But her body reacted by fleeing. She opened the hotel door, ran down the stairs, and threw herself into the street, dodging cars, trying to escape her husband. But he was an expert at ensnaring women, and he overtook her before she had run more than a few feet; he dragged her off to a room in some neighborhood whose location is still unknown to her.

"You're staying locked up here until you decide. Let's see if it's true that you'd rather die than obey me," he said, as he slammed the door closed, shattering Camila's hope for a life without violence.

\* \* \*

In the room, there was nothing but a mattress, a kitchenette with a one-burner stove, and a chamber pot in place of a toilet. That was it. Her diet was very strict: she ate just twice a day, in the morning and at night, and always the same thing: a glass of juice and a small *tlacoyo*, a stuffed tortilla dish common in the region.

The diet only varied when Armando would enter, accompanied by other men. Then, between several of them, they would squeeze Camila's mouth so hard that her lips would form a funnel, through which they would force her to drink liter after liter of beer. When she would wake up, still dizzy from the alcohol, she would find herself alone in the room, surrounded by broken bottles, half-naked, and with a burning sensation in her genitals.

Sometimes, the routine was interrupted by long sessions of pornographic movies that Armando would force her to watch and to act out in order to "train her." Or by angry appearances of him, sunken in alcohol, throwing punches that dented her nose, her ribs, her breasts; and beyond that, her spirit.

With every passing day in that room, Camila could feel herself waning. She stopped being herself. It wasn't her bones that broke, it was her emotional wholeness. If she didn't get out of there, she would die slowly. So one night, as Armando opened her door, she chose to survive.

"Alright, I'll do what you want," she muttered, defeated from the torment. A mocking smile disfigured Armando's face, who once again threw a short skirt and nearly transparent blouse at her. "Put this on; you start tomorrow."

There are two ways Camila remembers how much time it took Armando to crush her spirit: one of them is counting the months—three—she was locked away. The other is counting the change in her pants size: she entered her dungeon as a healthy size 34 and left it a scrawny 28.

\* \* \*

Camila's place of "work" was a hotel in the historic downtown area of Puebla, close to 14th Street. When she entered and walked through the lobby with its cheap baroque facade, the first thing she noticed were the dozens of men gathered against the back wall, examining the women like someone would when choosing a hunk of meat.

One of the women explained how the brothel worked to Camilla: the clients would choose their escort, pay for her, and take her to a room. Thirty minutes later, the woman needed to be downstairs to begin again the cycle that would repeat all day. It was important to know how to behave, how to speak to the clients, how to speak to the police, and, especially, how to avoid getting hit by the group of traffickers that Armando was a part of. Camila burst into tears, fearful and anxious, when she realized what her life had become.

"But I won't be here long; I'm going to escape," Camila confided to the young woman assigned to be her teacher. But rather than words of encouragement, the veteran looked at her with pity. "My dear, I said the same thing, and look at me...I've been trapped in this place for five years."

The sexual relations were so violent and frequent that Camila remembers how urinating felt like expelling hot sand. The dryness of her genitals contrasted with the moistness of her eyes, always ready to weep as soon as she hid in the restroom. She was never able to count how many times she was forced into sexual relations, but each one felt like a thousand rapes.

The autumn of 2006, when Camilla first arrived at the hotel, stretched on into the winter. Christmas, New Year's Day, and Día de los Reyes (Day of the Magi) passed. Every day was more grueling than the last. Valentine's Day, remembers Camila, was a special day: maybe it was the holiday or her mental and physical exhaustion, but that day she refused to go to the hotel. "It's Valentine's Day and I don't want to spend it there!" she screamed at Armando, who, furious, punished her as he always did: locking her in a room without food or water.

A few hours later, Armando came back, drunk and violent. He entered the room and let loose a blow that broke her nose. *That's enough*, she thought. The hate she felt for him put her senses on high alert; he, on the other hand, was numbed by beer. She seized her opportunity, grabbing a bottle and shattering it against the floor, and the bottle became a blade.

"I hate you! I hate you! Let me go or I'll stab

you, and I'll kill you!" she screamed, surprised by the strength of her own voice. The fragments of her shattered spirit had reemerged as a mosaic of bravery and survival. Camila managed to maneuver herself close to the door, then open it. As she was about to close it from the outside, Armando suddenly moved and gripped the door to keep it from slamming shut. But nothing could stop her from fleeing: she rammed the door and crushed Armando's fingers as hard as she could. To make sure his fingers were broken, she smashed them a second time; she heard a crunch, and she ran to the street.

Camila took advantage of the fact that Armando was writhing in pain on the floor to hide in an alleyway and wait for dawn. She didn't want any surprises at night. As soon as the sun came up, she took a taxi to the Puebla bus terminal. She stopped only once, to pawn off some jewels she had hidden in her shoes; with the money she paid the taxi driver, ordered a hot meal, and purchased a bus ticket to take her out of that hell disguised as a port of paradise.

Since she couldn't go back to her family in Guerrero, she chose the place on the map that seemed the most well-known to her: Mexico City.

\* \* \*

Without a cosigner to rent an apartment, Camila had to live in a hotel once again. She chose one in an urban neighborhood, centrally located and cheap, buried in the Venustiano Carranza area of town. She had been told she would be able to find work there, even though she didn't have legal documents or a residential address. When she moved in, though, her fears were confirmed: the only "work" available was to trade money for forced sexual relations in La Merced.

*Guerrero* is the Spanish word for warrior, but the fighting spirit of this girl from the state of Guerrero was broken. The money from the pawned jewels was disappearing quickly, and everything seemed to conspire against her, forcing her back into prostitution. Worn out, she resigned herself to once again putting on the short outfits, standing on the street, and waiting for clients. It was a dark, turbulent *déjà vu*, with one small difference that didn't make her feel any better: this time the money went to her, not her trafficker.

Three days after arriving at La Merced, a couple of girls from the street invited her to an event. The local authorities, working together with several foundations that fight sexual exploitation and violence toward women in difficult neighborhoods, were raffling household appliances to help women. In reality, the raffle was an excuse to get into the area without danger, to understand the social dynamics better, and to build trust in order to locate potential victims. From afar, it may have seemed what some would call populism; but, from the inside, it was the only way to infiltrate the neighborhood and rescue its prisoners.

The strategy worked. Camila won a microwave, but she decided not to claim it. Her sudden happiness evaporated when she realized she didn't even have a house to use it in. She went up to the event organizers to return it and to ask them to redo the raffle so another girl would be able to use it.

When she told them she lived in a hotel, it was as if she opened a box of secrets. And once opened, it was impossible to close. She revealed that she didn't like her room because it reminded her of the days she was held captive as a punishment for not giving in to the desires of her captor. And she did the most important thing: she didn't stay quiet. She broke the silence Armando had accustomed her to and blurted out, "I don't want to be here."

She didn't know it, but that morning she took the first step in transforming herself from victim to empowered woman. At the same time she took her stand, she was given a helping hand by a civil organization dedicated to the care of those who have suffered similar crimes. That is how Camila became the first woman rescued by Fundación Camino a Casa. There was reason to wait, so that same week she left the hotel and was placed in the closest thing to a home, where she could plug in the microwave she won the day she dared to renounce the false destiny that had once seemed inevitable.

Camila's steps towards recovery have served as a guide for the foundation to design a rescue model for dozens of other victims over the last ten years. Camila didn't just receive a home that wasn't a hotel room. She also received psychological, legal, and economic support; along with the accompaniment she was missing to rebuild her broken spirit. Thanks to the success of that protocol, many other victims have returned to a life without violence, with Camila as their example of survival and triumph.

\* \* \*

Today, Camila lives with her three children and a man who loves her; she is, against all odds, a successful micro-entrepreneur. With the help of Fundación Camino a Casa and her own abilities, she gained training, studied business models, and opened a beauty salon that is in its seventh year and is financially healthy. And she's not stopping there: her next dream is seeing her own children graduate from college.

Her soul became resilient. Her skin became harder, but not her heart. And her broken nose is just an old curve that gives personality to her face. She still has scars from the past upon which she is building her future.

Today, the only plastic bag—black, opaque, a little bulky, capped with a tight knot—that Camila carries is the trash bag, which she takes out after tidying up the business she owns, the greatest symbol of her recovery.

She looks at all she has built; she sits, smiles, and thinks to herself, *Camila, you're going to work today… and you're going to do whatever you want, because you are finally a free woman.*

*To view a Spanish-language news report about Camila's experiences, scan this QR code with your smartphone camera or app.*

# Long-term care of human trafficking survivors

During the first few years of work for our organization in Mexico, one of the biggest obstacles we faced was the lack of knowledge and awareness by those charged with law and justice. In reality, neither the police, nor public servants, nor the judges or prosecutors understood this crime. Today, it is a different story in several of Mexico's states, although training is still one of the growth opportunity areas highlighted by a recent study we conducted, which analyzed criminal trials; and there is much left to do to achieve the level of commitment from the authorities that we envision. I am happy to report that our country now has specialized, interdisciplinary human trafficking units who have trained by both national and international teams. And I would like to highlight the work done by the specialized federal police force, as well as the specialized prosecutor's office in Mexico City, who must be recognized for their progress in the understanding and persecution of this crime, including its impact on the lives of the victims and the importance of bringing to justice those who have imposed so much pain.

When I served as a congresswoman, I dedicated my time to ensuring that a strong and strict law would be passed to prosecute this crime and protect the victims. Today, 99% of the abusers of the victims we have helped have faced justice, with sentences ranging from four to ninety years; however, very few victims have received reparation for the damage from the State. Instead, it has been civil organizations like ours who have taken on the responsibility of repairing the serious harm done to the victims. My team and I devote a large portion of our resources to awareness campaigns for legislators, police groups, judges, and the general community.

One of the most important things we have been able to do is open a door for the voices of the survivors to be heard. More than sixty gave their testimonies to the legislators; a number of these legislators heard for the first time a live, firsthand description of the terrible consequences of human trafficking. The "General law to prevent, punish, and eradicate crimes in trafficking of persons and for the protection and assistance to victims of these crimes" was unanimously approved in the last few months of my term in the lower House. Since then, this law has helped provide a mechanism to carry out the national plan against trafficking, as well as to create "inter-secretarial commissions" (which currently exist in thirty states) who coordinate the work between the federal and state levels.

The law was written to take into account the specific context of Mexico, a nation categorized as a *source*, *transit*, and *destination* country for trafficking. Over the last seven years since this law was put into place, the legislation has run into fierce opposition due to its impact and to the fact many people don't understand its profound significance. When vested interests are affected, great opposition is to be expected. In the last four years, there have been attempts to reform the law in a way that would benefit traffickers and gravely affect the rights of the victims whom the law is meant to protect. Like all human works, this law can be improved; and although it must be strengthened even more, it is working. More than one thousand traffickers are in prison, and more than one thousand illegal businesses, cabarets, hotels, and nudist clubs where exploitation has been discovered have been shut down.

As I have already mentioned, this law has three different aspects: prevention, prosecution of the crime, and protection of the victims. It should be mentioned that in the third area as well there has been great progress.

The first couple who took responsibility for the legal side of things for the girls in the shelter were Germán and Lorena. Their lives were forever changed when they met their first victim, a sixteen-year-old girl, who told them everything in one short phrase: "I am trash." Germán and Lorena quickly realized they couldn't just provide legal and psychological support to these young women: they needed to provide a home and care as well as protection. Germán never forgot his reaction upon reading the first file given to him by the legal authorities. It was a cold, impersonal story of unthinkable crimes committed against a teenager. The documents couldn't capture the pain and lack of trust reflected on her face.

That is one of the biggest obstacles to overcome. How can you establish trust with someone who has had their soul destroyed? These young girls have been raped, violated, beaten, manipulated, and made victims to thousands of lies. This young girl in particular had suffered in captivity for more than four years. How could she survive so much sexual, emotional, and physical violence? The process was not going to be easy: the emotional and physical scars were still fresh in her memory, in her heart, and in her skin. What can bring healing to the girl who says, "God is nothing to me: he expects me to forgive them, and I never will"?

Since then, we have learned important lessons about the care and attention that a trafficking victim needs in order to heal and flourish. The importance of empathy, of honesty, of a respectful approach, and of persistence when a legal case gets held up, as was the case with this young woman. Unfortunately, it is often within the system itself that the heaviest doors close, and victims are revictimized through the arduous process of testifying again and again. Many times, the victims feel betrayed by the very system that is responsible for protecting them.

The processes to care for victims have become daily routines in our different programs of care and companionship. The shelters house up to twenty-five girls who are learning to live together, sharing responsibilities and privileges as any healthy family would. Each girl has her own experience, her own personality, and her own dreams. Making sure that respect reigns is of the utmost importance, as is showing them we will always be there to fight for their rights. We help them understand that the recovery process is a cycle which must be lived out; that recognizing they are victims is the first step toward accepting that what happened to them was not their fault; and that anger, depression, and shame are a natural part of the cycle. In other words, our priority is to help them feel and see that we will be patient while they live all of this out.

As you can imagine, working as a caretaker at a shelter is a huge job. Helping others recover a life of dignity is not just another job. Each member of the family needs time and a personalized program that is based on her specific needs. In these homes, there are many tears, but also much laughter and many rays of hope that keep the light of their dreams alive.

The shelter becomes a home and the members a family. Whether the members stay or leave, the family will always be there for them. This is where they first wake up from their nightmare, where they develop dreams and began to live them out. This is where they get an education, trauma therapy, physical and emotional healing, and security.

With the arrival of girls as young as six years old who have been prostituted out by their own mothers, we've implemented a special companionship program in order to provide love and care from people who will make them feel like they are part of a family, not an institution.

When we started over twelve years ago, few of us understood the real needs of the survivors. As time has passed, more than two hundred victims have passed through our doors, and many more people have joined the indispensable network of support. Together we have come to understand that long-term care is the best way to ensure successful reintegration, and there are many different people who help in important ways. Public servants and committed private citizens have been pillars in building the structure necessary for this family to become successful in what it does.

Today, using a model of care we call the "Virtuous Cycle," we are achieving success. The center of

Figure 5.1: Virtuous Circle
Comisión Unidos vs. Trata, 2019

this model must always be human dignity, which is precisely what was stolen from the victims of trafficking. When victims are rescued, it is clear that they are living with desperation, depression, and maybe even suicidal thoughts; or maybe they are profoundly enraged at the betrayal and pain they have suffered. Every person, especially the authorities responsible, must be trained to restore dignity from the first moment of contact: including the way in which a victim is spoken to; by assuring her that her words will be respected and taken seriously; by remaining patient while she recovers the strength needed to talk about what she has gone through; and by providing her with food, adequate clothing, and a dignified place to rest. In each step, she must know that she is being cared for and respected, not taken advantage of.

The first step after a victim is rescued is to make sure she is placed safely in a shelter that specializes solely in assisting survivors of human trafficking. This shelter should offer lodging, food, medical attention, social work, psychological support, legal advice, social and occupational support, and educational support. We call this a "Family Home." In our experience, it is best for the shelter to be run by a civil organization with the supervision and accreditation of the proper government authority. The homes are based on the idea that the safe return of the girls to their families—if that is the goal—or their path toward full reintegration into a productive social life starts with the values, experiences, and learning they acquire while at the home. The program also involves planning out various elements related to formation, values, education, and assistance which together give children and young people the foundations they need to rebuild and reshape themselves, both individually and in relationship to others. These can be divided into two main thrusts:

- *Life plan*: this is a strategy in which the girls

visualize, reflect on, and become aware of, little by little, the transformational process they are living on a personal level every day. It helps them clarify and develop their own qualities and potential, and it allows them to respond to the demands of the holistic care they are receiving.

- *Family plan*: This plan is laid out, organized, and executed within the Family Home, and it is designed collectively by all of the members who live there. This plan assigns tasks and responsibilities related to keeping the house clean and in order, managing the supply and preparation of food, and attending school, extra-curricular classes, and medical and psychological appointments. Here the members also agree to follow guidelines and basic rules of coexistence.

Once a survivor is eighteen years old and has demonstrated substantial recovery, she enters the next stage, which we call *Pasos Firmes* (solid steps), with the aid of Reintegra, along with support from Comisión Unidos vs. Trata, @SinTrata, and Fundación Camino a Casa. To continue with this step, the victim needs to be a "survivor," meaning she has received, for a sufficient length of time, the assistance she needs in legal, psychological, physical, medical, educational, and cultural areas, all meant to prepare her for the goals she wrote in her "Book of Dreams." Then the survivor, out of her own will, decides whether or not to enter the Pasos Firmes program, in which she chooses a professional or vocational career she is passionate about. During the time she is in school, we look for partnerships with local universities or with business owners who will help with scholarships, housing, and personal expenses. Besides this, on the legal side, we pursue the compensation and reparation of damages for her that she is entitled to by law.

During this time, survivors who choose to do so can prepare to become activists who tell their stories and work to achieve greater awareness of the suffering that victims experience and, more importantly, the achievements they can accomplish if they are supported and empowered. Another important aspect is establishing agreements with authorities and businesspeople to ensure the survivors will have good, dignified jobs after they have received their college or technical degree.

In addition to these efforts, it is important to ensure that public service workers—and society as a whole—are trained so that, when the survivor is reintegrated, she is not hurt or revictimized.

Another highly relevant aspect is educating society about the importance of reporting crime. This includes creating awareness campaigns that inform people about the characteristics and circumstances of potential victims and working to make sure there is a safe, reliable process to accompany the victim or accuser throughout the process necessary

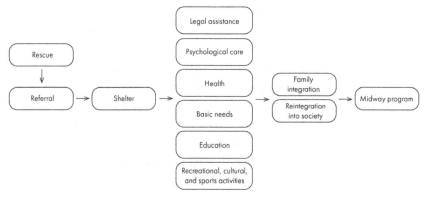

Figure 5.2: Care Model
Comisión Unidos vs. Trata, 2019

to ensure her care.

Putting the victim first is a team effort that helps this process be carried to completion. The survivor becomes an overcomer: she has a professional or vocational career, a meaningful job, physical health, emotional stability, and a dignified place to live. When she begins to be financially and emotionally independent from those who have accompanied her, she becomes justifiably proud of herself and what she has accomplished; and even more than that, she feels grateful, and she is committed to helping those who come behind her.

One important step is to educate people that when they repeat, normalize, and accept myths about the prostitution system that permeates our culture, they are contributing to the perpetuation of the crime. This includes phrases like: "It's the

world's oldest profession"; or, "They are there because they want to be"; or, "Prostitution is a necessary evil."

"We as men," Germán used to say, "have to
make structural changes in our culture to stop seeing women as objects of our pleasure and to stop
violating them sexually. We have an obligation to
build a society based on the values of respect and
equality. Our message should educate society about
the reality of human trafficking and fight for the
victims at all times."

## Chapter sources

Much of this chapter is excerpted from a Spanish article
titled, "Dignidad y éxito: el protocolo de reintegración a
largo plazo para víctimas de trata" (Dignity and success: a
long-term reintegration protocol for trafficking victims), by
Rosi Orozco, for Fundación Camino a Casa and Comisión
Nacional de Derechos Humanos. Used by permission of the
author.

Previously published in, among other sources, *Trata de
personas: un acercamiento a la realidad nacional*, P. Prado &
B. Casas, 2011, http://cdhpuebla.org.mx/pdf2019/
Acercamiento-Trata-Personas_1.pdf.

# VI. Esperanza, Mario, and Enrique: Restoration

*An empty house* can mean many things. For the fictitious detective Sherlock Holmes, an unoccupied house was always suspicious, a place of terrible crimes. For the Chilean novelist Carlos Cerda, an abandoned residence revealed pain and guilt from the past. Nietzsche said his ears hurt when he would enter an uninhabited home. And the Argentine singer-songwriter Charly Garcia dedicated an entire song to the concept in *Casa Vacía*.

For artists, poets, and creators, an empty house nearly always evokes pain, an open wound, a sign that disaster struck with force and erased all signs of love. For Esperanza, a girl from Mexico City, an empty house is the beginning of her story. A dark residence, tenuous, that never managed to feel warm or cozy as it stretched itself across a few square feet in the Obrera neighborhood in the heart of Mexico City. Esperanza looked for her mother there, but she never found her; she looked for her father, but he was probably working as the manager of a restaurant in Acapulco or Cancun. The house was empty almost all day long, even if she and her eight siblings had not eaten.

The house lacked love but had more than enough pain. From the age of five, Esperanza was beaten so badly that people seemed to want to break not just her bones, but her soul. She remembers walking to the corners of the house, rubbing her bruises, trying to understand how a mother could turn a home into a merciless cell of punishment.

Esperanza's empty house was also a dungeon. She would spend days and days locked up, watching sunny days pass by on the other side of the window. She would dream she was the little girl she could see outside crossing the sidewalk to play with other girls. She fantasized, for years, at the edge of that window, about the childhood others were living: one that included games, laughter, candy, pretty clothes. One day, an elderly neighbor spoke to her through the window. He showed her a piece of sweet bread to get her to come outside. Esperanza didn't trust the man, but her hunger and the desire to get out of the empty house pushed her out of the door, across the street, and into the old man's house, which, she remembers as if it were yesterday, smelled like mothballs. He sat her on his lap. As soon as she was close, he touched her genitals, he put his fingers in her vagina, he hurt her. She didn't understand and she couldn't defend herself. "If you tell your mother about this, she's not going to believe you. I'll tell her that you left the house and you'll see what happens to you after that," he said before he told her to leave his house.

If it's true what the Greeks said, that your name signifies your destiny, being named Esperanza— Spanish for *hope*—did little to help this girl who trembled in her house after being sexually abused, who had only wanted bread and a warm house. That's all: bread and a warm house.

\* \* \*

Esperanza began her period, for the first time, at eleven years old. In her mind, most mothers would be happy the day their daughter reached menstruation. She thought the bleeding meant she was now a woman, and she waited hopefully for her mother to explain, calmly and lovingly, the bodily changes she was going to experience.

Instead, a cascade of blows fell upon her. The empty house could also be a boxing ring, one in which Esperanza had no right to defend herself. Her mother grabbed her by the hair and beat her head against the floor with the same fury one would show against a thief who had hurt the family. "What have you done?" she screamed, while she crushed her nose with the sole of her tennis shoes. Fists and feet flew until her mother was out of breath.

The little girl felt pain all over her body; blood was coming from her nose, her ears, her mouth.

She cried. She shook with fear. *What did I do?* she asked herself.

"She is your daughter. Look what you've done to her," Esperanza's father chided her mother, when he saw her deformed face; but her mother just shouted louder. And he, a loving, absent, flimsy man, took the place her mother should have taken. "This happens to all women. At the pharmacy they sell things for this," he explained, clumsily, about her first menstruation.

Even when the house was occupied by mother, father, and siblings, it was still a silent house. Everyone seemed to look at her with scorn or pity. Esperanza only put up with this for a time. She wanted to feel calm, peaceful, free of the beatings. So she started planning how she could find in the cold streets the warmth her empty house was never going to give her.

\* \* \*

Sometimes, the empty house would fill up. And that was worse. Any change in the daily routine of that place seemed to be destined for evil against Esperanza. When the door would open and close, and she heard the chorus of laughing men, the girl would tremble. Hours later, Esperanza would be on the floor, made to eat her own vomit as a punishment for fighting back against her own brothers, neighbors, and her brother's friends, who would force her to perform oral sex on every man in the house.

Her abusers said the same thing as the neighbor who had abused her: "If you tell your mother, she won't believe you." Esperanza didn't know if these men knew, or if they just guessed, that her mother would break the silence of the house only to insult her: "You're crazy, you're stupid, you'll never be anybody." These words instilled themselves in every corner of Esperanza's mind and shut windows of opportunity to learn new things. She began to fall apart at school, to fail class after class, and to believe the horrible lie that she was, in fact, stupid.

In sixth grade, her mother warned her that if she failed another class, she'd kill her. Better dead than a bad student, her mother told her. And Esperanza failed again. But before her mother came home, Esperanza ran away. She took all her things and left to live on the street. She preferred the dangers of the street to the certainty of a coffin. And the house got a little bit emptier.

\* \* \*

Two streets away from her parent's house, there was a bus station. Esperanza walked there and took the first bus to another station. She got off that bus and boarded another. She spent the entire afternoon like that, from bus to bus, station to station. She was a twelve-year-old girl roaming dozens of streets in Mexico City with nowhere to go.

The sky got dark. The bus arrived at the first bus terminal, where she had started her journey, like a vicious cycle. A man approached her and told her it was time to get off. She answered that she had nowhere to go, that she had been orphaned. He took her to a hotel on the same street as the bus station. He paid for the room, just two streets away from her old house. That night, they had sexual relations.

He, Mario, was a twenty-seven-year old man; she was a girl of barely twelve. The warmth of the sheets kept her asleep until dawn. When she woke up, he had already left. Esperanza looked for Mario like a drowning person looks for a life jacket. She searched at the bus station, at the food stands nearby, in the streets of the neighborhood; but she couldn't find him. While she looked, she ate a taco or two that people gave her along the way. After a week of searching, the girl finally found the closest thing she had to a protector. But he turned around. He rejected her. He didn't want anything to do with her.

\* \* \*

Esperanza slept on the streets for a year. She survived with an instinct that was almost wild, an instinct incomprehensible to any twelve-year-old girl who has grown up in a full house, warm and protected. The girl slept outside of any business that had an overhanging roof, such as a bank or a restaurant. Sometimes she sneaked into the buses at the station and slept there. For her, that was paradise.

Food was another misadventure. The men  who were good would offer her broth or bread and not ask for anything in exchange. The men who were bad would give her food in exchange for taking a shower with them. The men who were the worst would offer her crumbs or a soda in exchange for beating her in the bathroom of an empty building. They would get turned on by making a young girl suffer. But Esperanza didn't mind the beatings that much. The ones from her mother hurt worse.

During this year on the street, she ran into her mother a few times. Sometimes, her mother would buy her coffee or dinner. She wasn't the same woman as before; she acted very cold, but at least she didn't beat her anymore. This encouraged Esperanza to move back home: one day, walking side-by-side with her mother, but in total silence, she returned to the empty house. She thought going back to that place would be worth a kiss. But that gesture of love never came.

\* \* \*

Months later, Esperanza left her empty house. Mario had been looking for her and, oddly enough, he offered to introduce her to his family. She lied, saying she was eighteen years old, when in reality she had just turned thirteen. But a life of mistreatment and the toughness of the streets made her look older than she really was, so Mario's father and stepmother gave their approval for her to move in with them in a neighborhood just two blocks from the empty house. Esperanza felt something strange, a funny tickle she couldn't explain, when she entered her new home and saw a bed, a little stove, two plates, two cups, and clothes. What she felt was happiness.

But that didn't last long. The next day, Mario locked her in the room and went to work. He told her it was to keep her safe. Six months passed like this. She never left, not even to take a walk. Because she didn't know how to cook, Esperanza would ask the neighborhood kids outside her window to buy her sweets from the corner store. Her new house had become her new dungeon. Just as empty and just as silent as her childhood home.

One day, Esperanza tried to cook something. The thirteen-year-old girl managed to short-circuit the burner on the little stove, sparking a fire. The room began to go up in flames, and fire threatened to spread to the entire neighborhood. Locked in, unable to open the door, she reacted like a scared little girl: she hid under the bed. The neighbors ran to help her, and they broke the lock and chain. They were able to save her life and put out the fire. That was the only way Mario realized the danger of locking her up. It seemed Esperanza's life always had to brush up against death in order to survive.

\* \* \*

One day, Esperanza blinked, and she was seventeen years old. Her adolescence was over, and her protruding stomach reminded her that she was about to have her first child, Mario. It must have been the pregnancy and her impending mother-hood that motivated her to beg Mario to let her look for her mother after years with no contact.

Esperanza began searching for her family. Her old neighbors told her they were now living in Ciudad Nezahualcóyotl, in the State of Mexico. She traveled there and found a house that was only half empty. Her brothers told her their mother was not there: she had traveled to Chiapas to claim the body of the oldest brother, murdered with a nine-inch blade. Esperanza was sad because this brother had never abused her. On the contrary, he had taught her to fight to defend herself. Heartbroken, she returned home.

Mario turned out to be a lazy man. He worked first as a bus dispatcher, then at a used-magazine stand. He earned so little money that on occasion Esperanza sold her blood just to eat. What he was lacking in vitality, he compensated for with flirta-tiousness. Mario and one of Esperanza's sisters had sexual relations. Yet Esperanza never complained nor left his side. It was enough for her that he didn't beat her as much as her mother had. And she for-gave him to the point of having his second child, Enrique, when she was nineteen.

Esperanza saw an escape in alcohol. Her bat-tered self-esteem, the certainty of her ugliness and stupidity, the pain from her childhood beatings—it could all be drowned in a bottle of tequila. When drunk, Esperanza felt fun, loving, and pretty. Alcohol gave her the courage to leave Mario, but it introduced her to a new boyfriend, Ernesto, who was as violent as her mother. That is how Esperanza had her third child; and then a fourth was on the way. She was living by inertia.

\* \* \*

After a party one night, Esperanza realized that Ernesto, drunk and drugged, was touching her first-born son. She took the child away from him and, instinctively, slapped him. He responded with a blow that threw her several meters and broke her nose, and he took the child away. To get her son back, Esperanza begged him for forgiveness and promised she would never confront him like that again. The next morning, she fled with a crooked nose, two black eyes, and a lump in her throat.

When she had her fourth child, a daughter, Esperanza's parents refused to let her live with them. She again resorted to living on the street, this time as a single mother of four. Mario and Enrique, her young sons, begged for money in the subway stations so the family could eat. If they didn't come back with money, she would hit them. She had become a hard, cruel woman, a carbon copy of her own mother, except gaunter, especially for her age. And instead of an empty house in the Obrera neighborhood, the new "house" was in a garbage dump in Ciudad Neza.

One day, Esperanza blinked and her daughter

was fourteen years old. She took her to the bar she worked at and introduced her as her successor. She had no doubt that for women of their condition, the only tool for survival was their bodies, so she pushed her own daughter into a life of prostitution.

\* \* \*

Esperanza and her children were as tough as wood and sharp as rocks. The mistreatment, the beatings, the life in brothels, and the mornings hungover with abusive clients had made them that way. So much so that they were known as a gang. "Los Garfias," they called them. "I am Satan. If anyone messes with me, I'll take them out," Esperanza often repeated. Her ongoing survival resided in her fame as a thug. She would puff out her chest with pride when she heard people whispering her fearful legend as she passed by. "Don't mess with Esperanza, she's not afraid of anyone," they said in the alleys. Her reputation went hand-in-hand with that of Mario, her son, who became famous in the neighborhood when he had an enormous image of *Santa Muerte*, the Saint of Death, tattooed on his back, aided only by tequila and cocaine.

The sexual exploitation network within her family did not last as long as Esperanza thought it would. One day, an anonymous report sparked a police operation, and the whole family was arrested. The next day, the family appeared on the front page of the newspaper *El Universal*. Above the photo of her, her two sons, and her daughter, was the headline, "The Lioness and her Cubs."

The Santa Muerte tattooed on Mario's back was not very miraculous: each member of the family was sentenced to eighteen years in prison for corrupting minors, pandering, criminal activity, illegal deprivation of liberty, and rape. Esperanza spent her first year in the Reclusorio Femenil Oriente (Eastern Women's Prison), then eleven years in the Preventivo Femenil Tepepan (Women's Preventative Center of Tepepan). Because she was hired to clean the prison, she received the benefit of an interprison visit once a week. That's how she kept in touch with her children and with a teacher, who recognized her potential for writing and empowered her. The girl who believed herself stupid and useless ended up being a prolific writer who created plays for other inmates to act out.

Esperanza's redemption came through writing. Mario's and Enrique's redemption came through reading the Bible. "Your God will not change me," she told her children, not trusting what they shared with her. They continued to challenge her during visits to her prison with phrases you may have heard before: "Jesus loves you; he gave his own life for you on the cross, and he was resurrected. Ask him, if this is truth, to reveal it to you." The words didn't resonate with Esperanza at the time, but one day in her cell in Tepepan, she had a personal encounter with a loving God who had transformed her children. She began to pray, and she felt an immense peace come over her body; she wanted to run, to jump, to shout.

Esperanza was soon baptized, and her two sons followed her example. Her prayers didn't seek a quick release from prison, but rather for freedom once her healing process had concluded. And it happened: Esperanza was set free on December 12, 2014. Months later, in an effort to correct the path her life had taken and to keep girls like her from ending up in sexual exploitation, she found work at Comision Unidos vs. Trata.

\* \* \*

An empty house can mean many things. So can a full house. Full of love and solidarity, a house becomes a home, a shared space, a shelter where one can be safe, a new homeland for a refugee.

If it's true what the Greeks said, that your name signifies your destiny, being named Esperanza helped this trembling little girl, who struggled all the way into adulthood, finally achieve the life she wanted and deserved.

Today, instead of a silent house, she and her children have a warm and loving home: a house full of dreams.

# Restorative justice

It seems unimaginable that human traffickers could be restored. The crimes they have committed are so inhumane, so devoid of compassion, so full of depravity and hate: how could anyone think it would be worth trying to save them?

Despite the obvious growth of exploitation among women, girls, and boys in the commercial sex industry, we still don't have enough data or qualitative research that analyzes the traffickers themselves. A thorough study of this topic would give us insight into the similarities and differences between traffickers and victims. Among the limited research that has been published is a study by Troshynski and Blank, who interviewed active traffickers in the United Kingdom; from this study we can highlight several predominant characteristics of traffickers.[1]

To begin with, the authors state that there are four distinct "roles" within the trafficking business.

1. The recruiter: the person in charge of identifying and ensnaring the victim.
2. The pimp: the person responsible for controlling and dominating the victim throughout her sexual exploitation.
3. The trafficker: the person responsible for transporting the victim to the different points of exploitation.

4. The mediator: the person with the connections necessary to ensure the business functions without problems or setbacks.[2]

Based on this list, we cannot as a society focus our efforts solely on prosecuting the recruiter: each of the participants is an exploiter and a necessary piece for the criminal system to work, which is why they must all be brought to answer before the law. In Mexico, in states like Tlaxcala, Puebla, and the State of Mexico, entire families have joined forces to build trafficking businesses, with each member assigned a specific criminal role.

One interesting fact (and something every single trafficker interviewed agreed with) is that the engine that propels their work is the demand from the clientele. This clientele doesn't have a specific socioeconomic profile: clients come from every context. The traffickers also unanimously agreed that the people involved in running this "market," in general, come from a very violent past, and they repeat those patterns to control their victims. According to their testimonies, violence has simply been a constant part of their lives. It's worth mentioning that, in each testimony, it is possible to confirm the influence of the global patriarchal system that establishes attitudes, customs, and traditions; these things, combined with a culture that discriminates against poverty and race, contribute to the perpetuation of misogynistic views that are advanced by the very men who are attempting to justify their actions. Under this false logic, women are perceived as sexual objects who exist to fulfill the demands of privileged men. The women, also, are often easily convinced to join the "business" in order to raise their social status and live a "freer" life. All of these reasons make it easier for a recruiter to find help from within the organization rather than from outside. That is how victims often become victimizers in order to survive.[3]

The first time I visited a trafficker in jail, I went with the goal of interviewing him to learn more about how he thought and acted; I did it to better serve the victims we care for. To tell you the truth, I was terrified. I saw him walking toward me from down the hallway, and my legs began to shake. When we spoke, he demanded to know why I had written a book about him. I immediately reacted by pounding my fist on the table with a courage that came from some unknown place, and I said: "You are not that important! I wrote one paragraph about you in my book." That was the first of many interviews I have had with traffickers who are serving their sentences in prisons in Mexico City. What I have discovered throughout this process is that they also have a story to tell. Most of their stories are filled with violence, life on the streets, absent parents, abandonment, and much more.

For a while I would visit one trafficker who, for our purposes, I will call Pedro. He was the exploiter of one of the young girls who was halfway through our program, a girl named Paty. Ever since I was a young girl, I learned we should face our fears; and the greatest of my fears at the time stemmed from the fact that Pedro, who was sentenced before the Ley General vs. Trata was instituted in 2012, was soon to be released. Paty is one of our most outstanding young women; she had finished her law degree and was working on her master's in business and social entrepreneurship. Now she was at risk, which is why I found it necessary to visit the prison. After many visits and deep talks with Pedro, he asked me if it would be possible to have an opportunity to ask Paty for forgiveness. This meeting was documented by CNN in the video "Mercancía Humana" (Human Merchandise; see QR code below).

It was a transformational experience to be a witness to this act of repentance, but it was especially liberating for Paty, who today has become a strong and mature woman who is blazing trails for other survivors. She works to prevent trafficking as the honorary president of Comisión Unidos vs. Trata and as a lawyer, dedicating her time to help raise awareness among members of the legislature and giving conferences around the world.

I've been especially moved by the story of the Garfias family, who now have a special place within Unidos vs. Trata. They actively support the fight against trafficking by giving training to prosecutors and judges, teaching parents about the dangers of this crime, and educating people on the various recruiting and exploitation strategies that traffickers use. Their involvement is especially important because of their firsthand understanding of sex-trade dynamics, having once been exploiters of women themselves. Recently their experience was shared in a documentary by the Thomas Reuters Foundation, "Sex Trafficking, A Family Business" (see QR code below). It's a story worth hearing: no one is beyond hope; no one is past restoration.

*Mercancía Humana (Spanish)*

*Sex Trafficking, A Family Business*

*Scan the QR images above with your smartphone camera or app to see the videos mentioned in the story.*

# References cited

1. Troshynski y Blank, "Entrevistas con tratantes," Percepciones, 2003/2014. https://cap-press.com/pdf/heil-nichols-online-chapter-01-Troshynski.pdf.
2. J.K. Blank, "Human Trafficking, Migration, and Gender: An Interdisciplinary Approach," 2013, M.W. Karrake, *The Other People: Interdisciplinary Perspectives on Migration,* New York, NY, Palgrave Macmillan.
3. Dina Siegel and Sylvia de Blank, "Women who traffic women: the role of women in human trafficking networks," Dutch cases Global Crime, Volume 11 (2010), https://www.tandfonline.com/doi/abs/10.1080/17440572.2010.519528.

# VII. Estrella and Carla: Understanding

*A semitrailer drives* along the highway that connects the State of Mexico and Puebla. It changes from lane to lane, passing cars that move more slowly down the road. Seen from above, the semi advances like any other; perhaps in a bit more of a hurry than most, but it doesn't stand out from the mass of vehicles traveling the road.

It is a generic automobile. A semitrailer without personality. There is nothing different about it— except that, in the cargo area, thrown on the floor like bags of clothes, are two young girls, kidnapped and unconscious.

It would be impossible for drivers who pass by the semi to know this. From the perspective of other drivers and passengers, all that is visible is a tall, closed trailer that could be carrying coffee, or vegetables, or the household items of a family moving to a new city. The truck covers hundreds of miles without arousing suspicion: it drives through towns, passes inspection points, and even encounters police cars from time to time, who pass the truck without incident, unaware that mere inches away travel a pair of missing minors.

The semitrailer drives from early in the morning until dawn the next day. The prick of the sun and the swaying of the vehicle rouse one of the girls from her trance. She looks all around her; instead of the walls of her bedroom, she sees the steel sides of the trailer. She tries to think, but she can't recall how she got there, and she has no idea where they are going or who is driving them.

All she knows—a realization that strikes within seconds—is that life as she has known it is about to be over. And the only thing she can do is scream as loud as her voice allows: a shriek desperate enough to make a person's blood run cold, if only anyone were able to hear the terror of this teenage girl.

Didn't anyone hear the scream inside of that trailer? Did anyone listen to the terrifying shriek but decide to ignore it? Why did she scream for minutes on end, but no driver helped her?

Why?

\* \* \*

Every year in January, Tepetlixpa, a small town in the extreme southeast part of the State of Mexico, hosts a festival to honor the Sweet Name of Jesus. The entire town is caught up in the anniversary. Grandparents, fathers, mothers, boys, and girls, just like fourteen-year-old cousins Estrella and Carla, look forward to the festival for twelve months.

The year is 2011, and the two young girls go to

the town center to enjoy the dancing, listen to live music, and eat until they feel like they will explode. These are the best days of their lives. They have nothing to worry about except enjoying the dazzling lights and the music of the festival.

They feel happy and free until they see the time and realized it is after nine o'clock. Estrella is afraid that her dad is going to be upset with her, and her perfect day will be ruined; so she asks Carla if she can stay at her house to at least postpone the reprimand.

The two cousins start walking along the side of the highway. They have done this before, and usually someone from the town passes by and drives them closer to Carla's house. But that night the festivities captivate the town's attention, and the road seems deserted, dark, and dangerous.

Suddenly, Carla lets out a small scream. Shadows appear to climb out of a semitrailer parked along the edge of the road and begin approaching them. When the cousins try to react, it is already too late. The shadows are behind them; they have white cloths which they hold over the girls' noses and mouths. In seconds, Estrella and Carla become rag dolls thrown into the darkness of the trailer.

Carla is the first to awake. She doesn't know what has happened, so she screams as loud as she can, but the vehicle that carries her to an unknown location doesn't stop. She screams so much, and so loudly, that Estrella regains consciousness. She is so dizzy from the narcotic that she can't even scream.

In silence, Estrella crawls to a small grate in the trailer and looks out. She notices they are driving through the streets of San Juan Acozac, Puebla, a detail that will be very useful to her later.

Each cousin is trapped in their personal hell. Carla doesn't stop screaming and Estrella is as mute as a rock. The two girls don't know what to think when, finally, the truck parks, and the shadows who had captured them turn into men who push the girls toward a house. A woman emerges and gives them a handful of bills.

Neither girl has any doubt that the money is payment for their kidnapping.

The woman introduces herself, in a condescending tone, as Jazmin. If it weren't for the fact that she paid to have them kidnapped, the cousins might have thought she was a nice person. It sounds almost believable when Jazmin tells them that they will be good friends and that she will treat them kindly. Jazmin turns out to be an effective interrogator: in a matter of minutes she calms the girls' fears and obtains valuable personal information from both of them—which she will later use against them, by threatening to kill their families. Afterward, as another way to terrify the girls, she separates them.

"Now you're going to work for me," Jazmin decrees. She orders Estrella into the house of a woman who does a cosmetic transformation on her, changing her hairdo and makeup; then she throws her a miniskirt, a low-cut blouse, and heels that are too big. The young girl, furious, rejects the clothes. Immediately Jazmin drops her kind exterior and slaps her angrily, as if she had hated her since the day she was born.

"If I went through this, why can't you?" yells Jazmin, just as her boyfriend walks into the room. Estrella will learn this later, but he is the true trafficker. The earnings from the forced sex work end up in his pocket, and Jazmin is just a mid-level player in his organization. But at the moment, she seems fearful and murderous. "I kill the girls who don't obey," she growls. "If you want to go home, bring the money I demand and maybe I'll let you go."

At nine o'clock that night, twenty-four hours after she was kidnapped, Estrella is taken to an unrecognizable bar. She is assailed by the smell of alcohol and tobacco, the strident music, and the wandering gaze of clients who watch the women and girls with lustful, clouded eyes. Estrella looks for Carla, but doesn't find her. When she asks the other girls about her, one of them tells her it's better to forget about her cousin; Jazmin and her boyfriend have operations in Veracruz, Puebla, and Tlaxcala. "Who knows where they might have dumped her?"

The first client, the first exploiter, sits at her table. Estrella tells him her age, looking for compassion and protection. Instead of that, she notices with disgust that the fact she is a minor has caused the man to have an erection.

\* \* \*

Jazmin and her boyfriend are operating a large sex exploitation business. They obtain false documents for the victims and send them to bars whose owners know the girls are kidnapped and underage. There is a security system that operates twenty-four hours a day and knows their every movement: from how many drinks they offer clients in exchange for sitting in their laps to how many sexual relations occur. Nothing escapes the gaze of the guards.

The criminal ring also has what is known as a "safe" house: locked and guarded, it is anything but safe for the victims. It is close to the bars, behind a general store; six rooms jumbled together, rented from an elderly woman who knows perfectly well what Jazmin and her boyfriend use them for. The safe houses are an open secret in the unknown town where Estrella is held captive: neighbors, truckers, police, and entire families are aware that the girls from the bars are trapped in this place.

Estrella and the others work twenty hours a day for two weeks straight. Then, they are allowed twenty-four hours off. They shower at the bar since the safe house lacks showers or beds. They take care of their needs in the same room, in front of the other girls, leaving urine and excrement in a corner. When the girls are given food, it is rotten. The drinking water smells like sewage. The only reason they put up with all this is because they are forced to take drugs. How else could they survive two entire weeks drinking, smoking, dancing, being raped from one bar to the next, in at least five different criminal establishments?

There is no one, in any of the bars, whom Estrella does not ask for help. Waiters, guards, cooks. Everyone ignores her. When she asks one lady for assistance, believing she will help her because she is a woman, the answer is, "Jazmin knows what she is doing." She also begs the clients, but no one is interested in seeing her as a person, only as an object they paid for.

A month passes in this way until, in a cruel twist, Estrella runs into Carla in a bar. She discovers Carla was sent to Minatitlán, Veracruz, but she has returned to Puebla for the grand opening of a new bar. Estrella goes up to her, hugs her, kisses her. But Carla is not the same. She is cold, hard, painfully thin, full of bruises. She babbles something about being happy because she's fallen in love with Jazmin's brother who will take her out of this hell. Estrella doesn't have the heart to tell her that this is another one of the lies the ring uses to subdue their victims.

Estrella and Carla grow apart. The first one fights to find an escape from her hell; the second one has resigned herself to it. Estrella's only friend is another young girl who, when no one is watching, encourages her to follow her dream. "Escape, friend; it's better to risk being killed than to spend five years in captivity, like I have."

* * *

A month and a half after being kidnapped, Estrella escapes. She sees an open door, a distracted guard, and a clear path to flee, and she runs toward freedom. When she sees a police car, she waves her arms and gets the officers' attention. She tells them that she has just escaped after being kidnapped for a long time, and she begs them for help. The officers open the door and tell her not to worry, that everything is over. The patrol car starts up and drives through the town. Estrella feels a cramp in her stomach when the vehicle stops in front of the same bar she just escaped from. A blow knocks her to the ground, and when she raises her eyes, Jazmin is standing there, furious. "You can't escape. Here, everyone knows everything," says her trafficker. "You are going to suffer as much as I have, or more."

Security becomes stricter following her failed escape attempt. And the violence takes a toll on her body. Estrella starts to believe death would be best. Then, one night, she steals a glass of clean water. When asked the question, "Who took that glass?" her best friend lies: "I did it." Immediately Jazmin orders her to be savagely beaten. The child dies in front of everyone and Estrella, inexplicably, feels a sudden desire to survive and to tell the world what is happening there; she wants to save the others, to rescue her cousin. So she sharpens her gaze, her ears, every sense, to find an opportunity. And she finds one.

Behind an old piece of furniture in one of the bars, she finds an emergency exit without a chain. She doesn't think twice. She flees, avoiding the police. She runs as far as she can until she finds a woman who takes her out of town; then she finds six young people who buy her a bus ticket to Mexico City. There, lost among nine million inhabitants, she begs until she saves enough money. A mixture of fear and hope flood over her when she hands over her coins in the ticket office at the bus station. "To Tepetlixpa, please. A one-way ticket."

\* \* \*

At the street corner nearest her house, still dressed as a prostitute and with visible signs of having been drugged, Estrella breaks down in sobs. Doubts pierce her head: *How will I look my mother in the eyes? What will I tell her? Could she love me knowing I had sex with so many men?* Estrella knows that, even if she explains that she had been kidnapped, her mother will believe she was doing everything of her own will. But she prefers to take the risk, and she knocks on the door of her house.

Mother opens the door. The two weep and hug each other. Her sister joins the hug. Estrella asks to bathe, and she spends two hours in the shower because she feels so dirty. When she comes out of the bathroom, her entire family is in the living room. "Where have you been? What did they do to you?

Where is Carla? Why are you so beat up? Did you run away with your boyfriend?"

Estrella can't talk. She just cries, and cries, and cries.

* * *

After releasing her fear through tears, Estrella is filled with a justified rage. It's a useful hatred. A contempt which leads her to report to the authorities the names of her victimizers, the exact location of the safe house, the names of the bars, and the identities of the victims who had also been kidnapped.

The authorities carry out a raid in Puebla, and Jazmin, her boyfriend, and their accomplices are caught with drugs, money, and girls, including Carla. Seven victims dare to file a police report against the criminal ring. In just a few hours, the traffickers are in prison. But there is still a long ways to go before Estrella and Carla feel that justice has been served.

Estrella tries to go back to middle school. She wants to leave behind her kidnapping and sexual exploitation, but the principal won't allow it: he tells her to find another school because her story is a "bad example" to the other female students. She feels the same rejection from everyone in her town, so strongly that she attempts suicide three times.

Before a fourth attempt at taking her life, Estrella and I meet. It is November 4, and I call her, not knowing it is her fifteenth birthday. Her mother has been trying to find someone who can understand her. Fortunately, for me, we find each other; and I speak to Estrella over the phone. We agree to meet, and the connection is instantaneous.

Estrella immediately enters Fundación Camino a Casa, where she receives the psychological therapy she has been asking for. After three months in the program, she joins one of the programs run by Reintegra. The same thing happens for Carla.

Estrella's life changes completely; she travels to Rome and speaks in the Vatican at a summit against human trafficking, where she meets survivors from all over the world. In August 2016, Fundación Alas Abiertas Foundation (Open Wings Foundation), led by Karla de la Cuesta, donates a car to her. And the government of the State of Mexico gives her a taxi license so she can become an independent taxi driver, with the goal of having her own fleet of taxis.

Today, Estrella lives in Tepetlixpa. Other news and other events have come and gone, and the neighbors have forgotten her story, although there are some who still gossip behind her back. Either way, she doesn't pay any attention to the stares or the rumors. She has changed a lot: now she is mother to a four-year-old girl and a two-year-old baby boy. She has family, dreams, and a future.

And most importantly of all: she has her own voice, a voice that rings loudly, a voice that is impossible to ignore.

*Scan the QR images above with your smartphone camera or app to see the Spanish-language videos mentioned in the story.*

# Missing Women and Children

The quantitative data that addresses the abduction of minors and women in Mexico varies considerably depending on the source. According to the national registry of missing persons maintained by the Secretaría de Gobernación (Ministry of the Interior), between 2005 and 2017, 7,000 children and 9,000 women were reported missing in Mexico. On the other hand, civil organizations committed to supporting families with missing children report between 27,000 and 45,000 minors and 15,000 women have gone missing,[1] with an exponential growth rate of 974% in the last four years.[2] Another chilling fact is that 7 out of 10 missing children are girls.[3] The National Registry of Lost or

Missing Persons in Mexico, through April 2018, reports that 80% of missing girls are between 13 and 17 years old.[4] Trafficking networks often use child abductions to feed the demand for underage sex and child labor.

Findings published by the Red por los Derechos de la Infancia en México (Network for Children's Rights in Mexico) state that, especially during the sexennial of Mexican president Enrique Peña Nieto, 4,980 minors disappeared, 62% of whom were young girls. The organization asserts that this phenomenon could be related to various factors, principally to human trafficking crimes, sexual exploitation, and child trafficking, as well as the growing involvement of armed groups and organized crime. The two states with the most missing persons are Mexico and Puebla: between the two, they accounted for 40.5% of the country's missing minors during the last presidential sexennial. The municipalities that cause the greatest concern are Puebla, Tijuana, Ciudad Juárez, Monterrey, Hermosillo, Toluca, Culiacán, Matamoros, Ecatepec, and Nezahualcóyotl, in that order. The findings mention that in justice and law enforcement areas, the third most common category of crime against the rights of children includes precisely those crimes that affect their freedom.[5]

The study cited above by Toshynski and Blank[6] is emphatic in pointing out that the demand for sexual acts with minors is the motive behind the increase in kidnappings and missing persons. It is simple common sense that supply and demand will produce human trafficking of both minors and women. The fact that 90% of women in prostitution are victims of trafficking[7] means that of the 500,000 women in prostitution in Mexico, only 50,000 "chose" to be prostitutes. The number of men who are sexually active in Mexico is over 38.5 million (INEGI, 2015); of whom, according to the organization El Pozo de Vida (The Well of Life), 17% are consumers in the prostitution market, which equals 6.5 million men (not counting foreigners). Is it humanly possible for fifty thousand women to meet the demand of more than six million men? And, besides that, there is an increasing demand for sex with minors. One can only conclude that trafficking plays a huge role in the number of minors and women in prostitution.[8]

Mexico has moved forward slowly; however, two recent laws—the General Law for the Rights of Children and Adolescents, published in 2014,[9] and the General Law Regarding the Abduction of Persons—as well as the creation of a national database of missing persons in 2017,[10] together provide a firm foundation toward building the necessary policies to address these phenomena, which so deeply tear the fabric of society. However, as always, including with the General Trafficking Act, mere words on paper are not enough. The words must be backed up by the political will to act, starting with budgets. Unfortunately, official economic support, instead of increasing, has been experiencing reductions. Historically, laws have proven to be an effective engine of cultural and social change;[11] but for laws to succeed, they must be backed by true political commitment and enforced over the course of time.

## References cited

1. Arena Pública, "¿Cuántos niños desaparecidos hay en México? A ciencia cierta, nadie lo sabe," Arena Pública, 2017, https://www.arenapublica.com/. articulo/2017/06/05/5902 (Accessed 12-Sep-2019).
2. Católicas por el derecho a decidir, "Desaparición de las mujeres: una realidad en México," La Jornada, 2018, http://letraese.jornada.com.mx/2018/02/28/desaparicion-de-las-mujeres-una-realidad-en-mexico-5576.html (Accessed 12-Sep-2019).
3. H. Zamora Mendieta, "Desaparición de mujeres de 15 a 17 años subió 974 por ciento en cuatro años," *Cima Noticias*, Ciudad de México, 24-Feb-2017, https://cimacnoticias.com.mx/noticia/desaparicion-de-mujeres-de-15-a-17-anos-subio-974-por-ciento-en-cuatro-anos/ (Accessed 12-Sep-2019).
4. Secretariado Ejecutivo del Sistema Nacional de Seguridad Pública, Registro Nacional de Datos de Personas Extraviadas o Desaparecidas, RNPED, 2014-2018, https://www.gob.mx/sesnsp/acciones-y-programas/registro-nacional-de-datos-de-personas-extraviadas-o-desaparecidas-rnped.

5. Red por los Derechos de la Infancia en México, REDIM, "Balance anual 2018, análisis de coyuntura," 2018, http://derechosinfancia.org.mx/documentos/Balance_Anual_2018_2.pdf (Accessed 12-Sep-2019).

6. Troshynski y Blank, "Entrevistas con tratantes," Percepciones, 2003/2014, https://cap-press.com/pdf/heil-nichols-online-chapter-01-troshynski.pdf.

7. Fundación Scelles, "Prostitution: Exploitation, Persecution, Repression," *Economica*, (2016): 277 - 282, http://www.fondationscelles.org/pdf/RM4/1_Book_Prostitution_Exploitation_Persecution_Repression_Fondation_Scelles_ENG.pdf (Consultado el 14-June-2019).

8. P. Szil, "El papel de los hombres en la prostitución," Discurso presentado en jornada de formación sobre prostitución y mutilación genital femenina, otras formas de violencia de género en España, Aragón (2015), https://www.youtube.com/watch?v=f1kLIBLTYjw (Accessed 12-Nov-2017).

9. Diario Oficial de la Federación, Ley General de los Derechos de Niñas, Niños y Adolescentes, y Ley General de Prestación de Servicios para la Atención, Cuidado y Desarrollo Integral Infantil, Ciudad de México, 4-Dec-2012. http://www.dof.gob.mx/nota_detalle.php?codigo=5374143&fecha=04/12/2014.

10. Diario Oficial de la Federación: Ley general en materia de desaparición forzada de personas, desaparición cometida por particulares y del sistema nacional de búsqueda de personas, Ciudad de México, 17-Nov-2017, http://www.diputados.gob.mx/leyesbiblio/pdf/lgmdfp_171117.pdf.

11. Subham Chatterjee, "Is Law Really an Instrument of Social Change?" *Law Corner*, 2019, https://lawcorner.in/is-law-really-an-instrument-of-social-change/ (Accessed 12-Sep-2019).

# VIII. Karla Jacinto: Family

*Today, your name* is Karla Jacinto. You will be raped more than forty-three thousand times, beginning at the age of five years old, and the sexual violence will only intensify as you reach the age of twelve. You will suffer every unimaginable crime from a young age—physical abuse, sexual abuse, beatings, kidnapping, child pornography, extortion, threats—but you will also rise higher than many would think possible. You will transform from a victim into a survivor, and from there into one of the clearest, most powerful activists against human trafficking in the world.

Your journey will not be easy. You will be born in Mexico City, in a household where violence lurks in the walls. You will have an abusive mother and a father generous with his beatings. Before even entering elementary school, you will suffer a sexual abuse you don't want to think about very often, but one that will open a bitter wound in your loving personality, make you untrusting and sullen, and ultimately damage your relationship with your mother.

The irreparable wound from the sexual abuse, and your family's inability to halt that abuse over the next few years, will lead you to smoke cigarette butts you find in the street at the age of eight and to start drinking alcohol at the age of nine. It will be impossible for you to focus on school, and you will fail so many classes that you'll trade your backpack for a pair of roller skates which you'll use to roam the streets of Pino Suárez.

That's where you will meet Gerardo and his lying tongue, who will promise you that he is twenty-two years old, that he was born in Puebla, that he works as a car salesman; and that, like you, he has a violent and problematic family. You will feel empathy for him and give him a hug. You will give him your phone number. You will wait for his first message, and you will feel love—or what you think is love—when he asks you to go for ice cream and a walk. You will accept. And you will do so many times, until one day, Gerardo will tell you that Mexico City bores him and he'd love to show you how beautiful Puebla is. Your rebellion makes you accept. And you will feel, even though you're a little girl about to enter middle school, that you are free, independent, powerful; traveling alone with your boyfriend to another state without your mother knowing.

A girl like you, born into such an unstable home, will be surprised by the car Gerardo has in his garage in Puebla: a brand-new, bright-red Trans Am. You will also be amazed by Gerardo's united and loving family, including his cousins who tell you they have never seen Gerardo so in love. And you, of course, will feel butterflies in your stomach.

That night, at twelve years old, Gerardo will ask you to marry him. He will tell you that age is just a number, that he's convinced that you were meant for each other.

You will feel afraid, but not enough to stop you. After all the scoldings from your mother for coming home late, and truly believing that you're ready to be the wife of the man he appears to be, you will say yes.

Yes, Gerardo, I will marry you.

\* \* \*

In your life as a child bride, you will have everything you ever wanted. You will not cook, or clean, or do anything more than feel like the owner of this house in Puebla, which you now believe is your house, and you will dream about one day sitting behind the wheel of that beautiful red convertible.

But the dream won't last long. Gerardo will disappear for days at a time, and from the window, you will see how his cousins, who are your neighbors, bring into their homes a constant stream of suspicious-looking women. You will ask your new husband about it, and he will admit, without hesitation, that his cousins are human traffickers.

"What is that?" you will ask him.

And his response will calm you. "They make a living by taking care of girls who are prostitutes, but you don't have to do any of that."

You will believe him. But only for a time. Soon, Gerardo will tell you that money is scarce, and he needs you to work. You will offer to clean houses, wash clothes for others, or cook for the neighbors. He will tell you no, he already decided for you: you will be a prostitute, whether you like it or not.

You will cry. You will scream. You will refuse. But none of that will help you escape the plan that Gerardo has laid out for you: you will have a false ID and you will live at a hotel. And if you don't accept, you will suffer Gerardo's wrath. A woman, La Morena, will appear in your room and pull out a condom. You will feel disgusted as she explains how to put it on the penis of the clients who will exploit you; the positions you must bend your twelve-year-old body into; and your rates and times, as if you were an object.

You will want to reclaim your fairy tale. To say you made a mistake; that you agreed to marry and run away from home so you could live a happy life, full and free. But nobody will listen to you. And you will watch, terrified, twelve years old, as your first client opens the door of the room where you are trapped, smiles at you, closes the door...

\* \* \*

You will soon understand that being a child, in this illegal business, is almost a death sentence. The clients will know you are a minor; they will see you cry and beg, but they won't stop. You will watch your body wither away. No amount of makeup will be able to cover your eyes, swollen from inconsolable weeping. On top of that, you will know that Gerardo has guards watching you who tell him anything you do wrong, such as smiling at a client or spending longer than two minutes with him, things punished by beatings or worse.

You will know that there are other girls like you in neighboring rooms in the hotel. Girls who are forced to eat their own vomit. Girls who are burned with irons. Girls who are left for days without food. Girls who are beaten until their ribs are broken. Girls who are punished one day and never seen again. So you will not do anything except obey, to save yourself.

Gerardo will send you off to Irapuato as a sex slave. Later, you'll go to Mexico City, and eventually you will end up in Puebla. At each stop, you will feel as though you've experienced hell itself. You will know that, in order to keep up with the daily quota, you must force your body to work up to eighteen hours a day, even though they beat you, humiliate you, bite you. You will even survive attempted murder three times by men who find in the suffering of a minor an irresistible aphrodisiac, which they take back to their beds with their wives, and to their houses with their children.

At fourteen years old, you will get pregnant for the first time. You will miscarry the baby. You will get pregnant again. You will feel a powerful motherly instinct that your captors will cut off with one blow when they take your baby away and use her as a hostage against you, in case you ever try to escape.

You will lose all sense of time. Months will seem like days; years will barely be weeks. You will see clients from all backgrounds parade through the hotel rooms: students, workers, priests, criminals, hypocritical family men, and depraved foreigners. One day you will come close to a stroke of luck when the hotel where you are held captive is raided, but the federal cops will only rescue a few of the girls, and they will leave you abandoned in this pit, after raping you and photographing you naked.

You will feel a bitter urgency to die. You will feel alone, abandoned, as if you are always thirsty, and all you are offered are glasses of saltwater.

You believe nobody will help you...until you meet a man who is different than the others: José Victor Calvario Becerra, an older man who pays to be with you but who only wants company. He will tell you, over and over, that you deserve a better life, and he will encourage you to escape. Months later, he will help you plan your escape: he will tell you to ask Gerardo how much a day off would cost, and he will give you half of it. You will have to come up with the other half on your own, secretly.

One day, you will have obtained that seemingly impossible sum of money. Gerardo, happy with the massive wad of cash you give him, will even offer you your daughter for the day. "I want you back. If you don't come back, I will find you no matter what, and you will die with your daughter," your husband will threaten you. And you will respond, very seriously, that of course you will return, that you only want twenty-four hours of freedom, then you will return to your dungeon.

You will say goodbye to Gerardo. You will turn the corner on the street. You will walk to the bus station and buy a ticket to Mexico City. You will never go back.

\* \* \*

At sixteen years old, on November 11, two days after your escape, you will arrive at Fundación Camino a Casa. You will be picked up at the police station by a certain Germán Villar. You will arrive at the shelter holding your baby girl in your arms, and that is how you will meet Rosi Orozco and the rest of the counselors.

You will add up the numbers, the approximate sum of clients, from your years in captivity. The total will be more than forty-three thousand rapes. And you will feel hatred. So much hatred that you will constantly be angry. At the shelter, you will punch the walls, scream constantly, cry inconsolably, and even stop taking care of the daughter you love so much.

On the other hand, you will discover the most surprising unconditional love of all: that of strangers who give everything for people they don't know. You will find yourself surrounded by kindness, patience, and a new plan of attention for victims that makes your mental health a top priority. You will learn gardening, and digging your hands into the soil will do something magical in you. You will finish elementary school and middle school. You will be surprised to find that, with your emotional wounds covered with love, you are an excellent student.

You will begin to grow. Your wounds will heal. You will get your first job. Earn your first paycheck. Sleep your first nights without nightmares. You will earn the love and admiration of hundreds of people. You even manage to win posthumous recognition in Congress for José Victor, your rescuer.

And then, activism will enter your life. You will want to give yourself to the task of preventing other girls, boys, and young people from falling into the network of human trafficking. You will spend entire nights studying; you will practice in front of the mirror as if it were an auditorium; you will make yourself into a leader. And soon after, you will share your story bravely in front of television cameras, despite the fact that Gerardo is still free. You will not stop. You will give speeches and workshops at Unidos vs. Trata and Sin Trata. You will do this in Mexico, Panama, United Arab Emirates, India, the United Kingdom, and Argentina, and at the Vatican during the World Mayors Summit of 2015. Your words will help inspire the passage of the International Megan's Law, which helps prevent sex tourism.

You will be the face of Fundación Camino a Casa. But more than an image, you will become a vital cog within the organization. And you will have an enormous responsibility: to connect with the girls who are at the shelter and help them through their process. One survivor to another. You will move hearts, bring change, and speak for those who are unable to do so. You will prepare yourself to lead the next generation of activists against sexual exploitation.

They raped you more than forty-three thousand times, beginning at the age of five. But you will rise up forty-four thousand times. Because your name is Karla Jacinto.

*To watch an English-language video about Karla's experiences, scan the QR code above with your smartphone camera or app.*

# Child sexual abuse

Official statistics note that one in four victims of sexual abuse in Mexico is a minor; however the reality is that 83% of women in prostitution in this country were recruited through manipulation, lies, or coercion before they were eighteen years old. When we take into account the vulnerability index, it is important to reiterate—as I have multiple times in this book—that women and young girls are at the highest risk of falling into the clutches of human trafficking, especially if they were victims of physical or sexual abuse during their childhood.[1] Yes, poverty is a massive social problem that needs to be faced responsibly in Mexico; but child sexual abuse is a serious social depravity that must be eradicated before we can even consider preventing human trafficking. The OCDE lists Mexico as the number one country in the world in terms of childhood abuse, stating that 4.5 million children are currently suffering physical or sexual abuse in Mexico.[2]

Megan's Law was approved in in U.S. in 1994 in memory of Megan Kanka, a seven-year-old girl who was raped and killed by Jesse Timmendequas, a sexual predator who had moved to her community a few months prior. This law requires that all sexual predators register with the authorities, who, through a website, can inform neighbors if a sexual predator lives in their neighborhood. This allows the community to be aware of possible dangers and to take steps to protect their children. Unfortunately, in Mexico, the majority of childhood sexual abuse cases are not the result of people who are unknown to the victim; on the contrary, it is estimated that 60% of sexual abuse happens in victims' homes, of whom 4 out of 10 are younger than 15 years old. [3]

In 2015, congressman Christopher Smith invited the Mexican survivor Karla Jacinto, whose story you just read, to make a statement before the US Congress and to share her experience as a victim of trafficking, bolstering the argument that countries, as well as neighborhoods, need to be informed if sexual predators leave the United States and cross international borders. Karla testified that many of her "clients" were Americans who traveled to Irapuato with the sole purpose of having sexual relations with minors. She urged Congress to rise up and fight the international sale of girls and boys which is destroying lives on a daily basis. At the beginning of 2016, President Obama signed the International Megan's Law initiative requiring the United States to report when a sexual predator travels across its borders.

The World Organization of Tourism and Immigration states that 600 million people travel around the world every year, and 20% of these trips are for the purpose of sexual tourism; meanwhile, 3% of that group admits to having pedophilic tendencies. This means that up to 3.6 million people may be traveling the world with the specific intention to rape children every year. The seriousness and relevance of this fact to Mexico is that this country is considered by the same international organizations to be the second most popular destination in the world for sexual tourism, surpassed only by Thailand.[4]

## References cited

1.  Wright Clayton, E. Krugman, and P. Simon, "Confronting Commercial Sexual Exploitation and Sex Trafficking of Minors in the United States", 2013, Institute Of Medicine and National Research Council of the National Academies, The National Academies Press, Washington, DC, https://www.nap.edu/read/18358/chapter/3.
2.  Senado de la República XLIV Legislatura, Coordinación de comunicación social, 2014, http://comunicacion. senado.gob.mx/index.php/periodo-ordinario/ boletines/15298-mexico-primer-lugar-de-la-ocde-en-maltrato-infantil-senador-martinez-martinez.html.
3.  Alumbra, Early Institute, "El diagnóstico de la situación del abuso sexual infantil en un contexto de violencia hacia la infancia," 2018, https://www.dropbox.com/sh/ urr6iptpndjrfom/AAAVzr3pMZehMfYY-HY5_Gkga?dl= 0&preview=Diagn%C3%B3stico+Alumbra+ASI+- +Early+Institute+.pdf.
4.  Blanca Ivonne Olvera Lezama, "Turismo Sexual Infantil," Editorial Flores, Ciudad de México, 2013.

# IX. Luis Armando: Music

*A **seemingly harmless*** message travels across Facebook like a trail of gunpowder. No one who sees it could guess the suffering it hides. The photograph accompanying the text is a smiling boy, friendly-looking, maybe sixteen years old, who gazes into the camera while seated in a photo studio, barefoot, guitar in hand. It is an image that might adorn an album cover. Above the image is the name of the boy, Luis Armando; his emerging career: singer; and the promise that hiring him for your "special event" would be unforgettable.

Anyone who saw it would think it is an advertisement for a young artist trying to break into the world of music. Someone who discovered at a young age his passion for song and is determined to conquer the stage, step by step, little by little, one gig at a time.

But those who know the real intention behind the post understand that it is not promoting his music: he is being prostituted. The telephone number that appears in the ad for reservations is actually a number for booking a sexual encounter with the minor. The "special event" advertised will not happen in a restaurant, bar, or shopping center, but in a hotel room or in the house of a pedophile who pays the boy's promoter: a man named Mario, a trafficker disguised as a "manager" of child artists.

The Facebook post does not just hide the fact that, tonight, Luis Armando, at sixteen years of age, will be forced to take off his clothes in front a man who cares nothing about his talent. It also hides a terrible reality that is not immediately obvious: men can also be victims of human trafficking.

\* \* \*

Armando is a boy with innate talents, the kind one is born with and then refines from a young age. His talent is singing. Life gave him a voice that is potent, pristine, with a warm intensity; a voice that quickly made him stand out in the choir at his music school and that took him to the television channel Televisa del Golfo, in his hometown of Tampico, Tamaulipas, when he was barely twelve years old.

The boy became fascinated with movie and television sets. The lights, the cameras, the microphones. The possibility of reaching thousands of people with his voice. He would step on the stage and feel an electric charge run through his body. When he performed in a musical and saw the power his voice had to produce applause and excitement, he knew the stage was his place in the world.

At fifteen years old, all Luis Armando wanted to

do was finish high school and pursue an education in music. He wanted it so badly that when he received a Facebook message from a certain Mario, who introduced himself as a producer of musical magazines, Armando believed it was his energy that had brought about the invitation to participate in Mario's talent academy.

Luis Armando's mother shared his enthusiasm. She supported him as he signed up for and participated in voice classes. Mario, the producer, had nothing but praise for his pupil's voice. Luis Armando's talent was so impressive that he soon began receiving offers to sing on stages in Madero, Tampico, and Altamira, as well as at private parties and cultural events. The two of them, adult and teenager, began building Luis Armando's musical career as a ballad and pop soloist. The dream was materializing.

But a terrible incident changed everything, Luis Armando's mother was kidnapped in Tamaulipas. After the ransom was paid, the criminal group that had captured her made her move to another state, so she fled to Nuevo Leon. Luis Armando would have been forced to quit school, cutting short what seemed to be a promising start to his musical career.

Facing the risk of losing Luis Armando, Mario acted quickly and offered to share his house with the boy. Because of his good relationship with his mother, he obtained her permission. Mario assured her he would be responsible for Luis Armando and care for him like the child he never had. The teenager's talent, he entreated her, could not go to waste. Luis Armando and his mother excitedly agreed.

At first, everything went well. The young boy was excited about his newfound independence and the personal attention he received from his producer, who trained him thoroughly. The intensity of the lessons, Luis Armando was convinced, was because Mario was so sure of his talent. Luis Armando was soon to be a star.

But one day, Mario asked him to arrive at one of the building of the academy an hour before rehearsal started. When he arrived, Mario surprised him with an odd request: to take off his shoes and socks and let Mario kiss his feet. A sensation of guilt, complicated by the gratitude he felt toward his teacher, caused the adolescent to give in.

From that moment on, everything changed. The apartment where Luis Armando lived alone, which was paid for by Mario, soon had to be shared with the producer. The teacher-student relationship transformed into a twisted friendship which began to take on romantic, disturbing tinges. Sometimes, Mario seemed more like a jealous boyfriend than a manager: he would go through Luis Armando's backpack to make sure nobody was talking to him, and he would force Armando to give in to his whims, like tying his hands and feet to the bed and sexually abusing him.

One day, Mario found messages on Luis Armando's cell phone between him and a girl he was dating. This discovery enraged the producer. The touching that once seemed affectionate became obviously violent. The relationship became one of slave and master. Luis Armando was subjected to sessions of sexual abuse that lasted two to three hours. He was made to watch pornography, and then, when he was aroused, forced to penetrate his abuser.

Luis Armando didn't tell anyone. First out of shame, but also because Mario controlled him by getting him gigs as a singer. *Maybe,* he thought, *someday, I'll become so famous and make so much money I can escape this abuse.* But the teenager never saw a dime. All the money he was supposedly earning with his voice went to Mario.

When Luis Armando threatened to quit the academy, although not his dream of singing, Mario responded with threats. He swore, if Luis Armando abandoned him, to use every one of his contacts to blacklist him every way he could. Defeated, Luis Armando continued to tolerate the emotional and sexual abuse.

One afternoon, Mario asked Luis Armando to participate in his first photo shoot, which, according to Mario, would help strengthen the boy's career as an artist. He ordered him to pose half-naked, arguing that sex sells in the music industry. He shot portraits of him in suggestive poses. A few days later, those same photographs circulated through the Facebook accounts of hundreds of pedophiles in the area. It wasn't long before Mario ordered Luis Armando to accompany him to Reynosa, Tamaulipas, where a client had paid to tie him up and abuse him.

Luis Armando doesn't know how many times he was forcibly prostituted by Mario. He only knows that within a short time, Mario was "promoting" Luis Armando not just in Tamaulipas, but in Nuevo Leon, Mexico City, and Veracruz, and that the clients were more and more violent. They would tie him up and do terrible, painful, humiliating things. Every penny, Mario promised, was accumulating in a fund to pay for his first album. According to the producer, that is how things in the music industry worked. If Luis Armando complained or tried to quit, Mario threatened to accuse Luis' mother of robbery and have her thrown in prison.

But Luis Armando's talent remained intact. Despite the abuse, his voice was still a gift. One day, the musical director of a band approached him personally and told him he was aware of his story and what was happening with Mario. He said he would help by paying him directly, rather than paying the producer, to sing at an event. And that—having his own money—empowered eighteen-year-old Luis Armando to do what seemed impossible: leave Mario.

"Do what you want to me and my family, but I'm not going to put up with this hell any longer. I don't want to work with you or be with you. I'm going to find my own career opportunities," he shouted. And to the producer's surprise, he left and found shelter with his mother and his family.

In 2014, Luis Armando was accepted on the reality show *The Voice México*, and he became part of the team led by the famous singer Yuri. Thousands of miles away from Mario, he felt safe. But not even that could stop the harassment. One day, the lawyer for the show called Luis Armando into her office to ask him who this demanding man was who kept asking for him. Luis Armando told her that he was his old manager, but that Luis Armando no longer had any contact with him. The lawyer made him publicly distance himself from Mario because, all the way from northern Mexico, the man was asking for money from his contacts using the name of Luis Armando and *The Voice México*, supposedly to cover the boy's personal expenses.

The public rift only strengthened the monster. Mario, furious, started a smear campaign against Luis Armando on social media. Like a wounded animal, he attacked whatever he could: his sexual orientation, his reputation, his mother, his grandmother, and even the woman the young singer had recently married.

Worst of all, Mario attacked him by publishing intimate photos of Luis Armando. They showed him naked, bound, in bed with clients. The pain, the rage, and the shame were impossible for the young singer to hide while he was on the show, and Yuri noticed his anxiety and promised to introduce him to me.

Thanks to the courage of Luis Armando, we were able to file a criminal complaint against Mario in early 2017. It was difficult work: delivering evidence, looking for witnesses, and remembering every detail as part of the trial in which the responsible, committed work of the authorities in Ciudad Victoria, Tamaulipas, played a decisive role.

Mario was arrested at the Tampico bus station as he was about to travel to Mexico City to work with other children in a musical. The authorities detained him while he was waiting for his bus, and his face fell when they read him the reason for his detention: human trafficking. Today, this trafficker with a rotten artist soul is incarcerated in the Penal de Altamira, in Tamaulipas, one of the toughest prisons in Mexico; and he has been sentenced to twenty-five years in jail for the crimes of rape and human trafficking.

Luis Armando, on the other hand, lives in Mexico City with his wife and their new baby; they are a young, loving family staying in a temporary apartment that Comision Unidos vs. Trata arranged for him, along with psychological therapy.

There, safe from Mario and the demons he unleashed, Luis Armando practices singing every morning. His vocation is still intact. No abuse was heartrending enough to separate him from his music. He still dreams of being on stage and hearing thundering applause, the spotlight trained on him in the center of the platform, giving himself to an audience that adores his talent. With that in mind, he continues studying. He might not recognize it, and it hardly seems possible, but his voice has only improved. His tone is more compelling, powerful, clear.

He would say it is from years of practice. The

rest of us agree, but we also know it has improved for one powerful reason: Luis Armando's voice has been made better by freedom.

*To watch a Spanish-language video about Luis Armando's experiences, scan this QR code with your smartphone camera or app.*

# Men are also victims of human trafficking

The global report on human trafficking by the United Nations Office on Drugs and Crime shows that between 2004 and 2016, the detection of male victims of this crime increased dramatically. In North and Central America, the average percentage of victims who are male is 18%, while the worldwide percentage is even higher, 25%. The majority of these men are exploited through forced labor and other work-related abuse, although there are more and more cases of men forced to participate in criminal activities. With reference to sexual exploitation, women and girls continue to be the most affected; however, boys make up 4% of those who have been victimized. The average age of boys who are sexually exploited is eleven years old.[1]

The American Psychological Association has published findings related to the vulnerability of men who fall victim to human trafficking rings. They discovered that the greatest number of cases occur in connection with the emotional needs caused by abandonment and rejection. As is the case with women who are ensnared, traffickers pretend to fill that need by offering friendship, shelter, and companionship; usually, this quickly turns into a relationship that involves drugs and alcohol. It is common for traffickers to become pseudo-fathers to the young men, creating an even closer relationship that is difficult to break later because of the loyalty that exists between them.[2]

Over the last few years, Mexico has paid more attention to the trafficking networks that are selling males. In 2017, Unidos vs. Trata opened the first shelter for men on the entire continent. A few months later, the United States opened two shelters for boys in North Carolina and Florida. In our shelter, boys between the ages of eight and fourteen live with their caretakers full-time and receive love, companionship, and support from them throughout their journey toward restoration and healing. They are also given psychiatric and psychological therapy, education, medical attention, legal assistance, and opportunities to participate in sports activities. As with the girls, we are learning as we go along how to give the best support to these boys who under other circumstances would have easily been abandoned by the system.

We have realized that many factors complicate this subject, including social stereotypes that make it difficult for people to see men as sexual victims. The idea that a boy should be able to defend himself makes it hard for people to understand that boys can also be coerced and deceived. We have seen firsthand how the boys distrust those who try to help them at the beginning of the process; since they depended so completely on their traffickers to meet their emotional needs, they now feel violated because they are separated from something that gave them a feeling of security, even though it also caused them pain. These ideas about "manhood" often inhibit progress if the victims aren't aware of the issue. Working with boys must include reinforcing their identity, resilience, unconditional love, balanced responsibility, and education. We have found that participating in sports helps greatly during the recovery process. When they experience opportunities for triumph and success, they are able to build confidence in themselves, which uproots the things that emotionally bound them to their traffickers.

There are no "official" protocols for helping male victims of sexual exploitation. We are writing them as we develop them, since the lack of care for this group is a global issue but there are few references to draw upon. The manual is being compiled with each new smile, and knowledge is built with the awakening of every fresh dream.

The emotional upheaval these boys and men suffer is overpowered by the family environment created by those who run the shelters. A new facility for boys was recently opened in Tijuana, directed by the International Network of Hearts, to work with the brothers of the girls who are cared for in their shelters. Many more are needed if we are going to adequately meet the demand. It is our dream that more people will rise up to face this great need and that there would be, at the very least, one shelter in every state in Mexico for girls, and another for boys.

# References cited

1. United Nations Office on Drugs and Crime, "Global Trafficking in Persons Report," February 2009, https://www.unodc.org/documents/Global_Report_on_TIP.pdf Accessed 12-Sep-2019.

2  Fairley Raney R., "Unseen victims of trafficking." American Psychological Association, Volumen 48, No. 24, 22, April 2017. https://www.apa.org/monitor/2017/04/sex-trafficking.

Figure 9.1

# Shelters in Mexico, by state

Shelters that specialize in caring for human trafficking victims

| With a shelter | Arrangements with another shelter | Without a shelter |
|---|---|---|
| Baja California | Coahuila | Baja California Sur |
| Colima | Michoacán | Campeche |
| Mexico City | Morelos | Chihuahua |
| Chiapas | Tlaxcala | Durango |
| State of Mexico | Tabasco | Guanajuato |
| Puebla | | Guerrero |
| | | Hidalgo |
| | | Jalisco |
| | | Nayarit |
| | | Nuevo León |
| | | Oaxaca |
| | | Querétaro |
| | | Quintana Roo |
| | | San Luis Potosí |
| | | Sinaloa |
| | | Sonora |
| | | Tamaulipas |
| | | Veracruz |
| | | Yucatán |
| | | Zacatecas |

Fuente: Comisión Unidos vs. Trata, 2019

# X. Madaí: Justice

*I met Jorge* during the summer of 2010, while I was living with my brother in Acayucan, Veracruz. I was in my second semester of a bachelor's program in educational psychology. As a university student, I never thought human trafficking could affect my life. I thought it was something that only happened to young girls and indigenous women without formal education. I was wrong.

One night, I was sitting on the curb, waiting for my sister-in-law to pick me up. Out of the blue, a man approached me and asked, with a deep, calming voice, if I knew where the dance was. I responded that I didn't know anything about any dance, and he smiled at me. He kept flirting, then he asked me my name and phone number; and I innocently gave it to him.

When I think about that first encounter, Jorge appeared to be about twenty-five years old; he was wearing athletic clothes and smoking a cigarette. I also remember feeling an inexplicable fear when I stood at his side. A fear that, without a doubt, I should have heeded during the next few years.

\* \* \*

One night, near Acayucan Park, my cell phone rang. "It's Jorge, we met that day...," he told me. The tone of his voice inspired my trust. I was bored, and his conversation kept me company. Jorge told me that he lived in Puebla with his family, that his grandparents had a ranch in Guadalajara, that he sold clothing for a living. We talked for a long time, and from that day on, he called me daily, usually at night, to ask me how I was and what I was doing, and to say nice things to me.

Three weeks after our first encounter, he asked me to be his girlfriend. At first I told him I would think about it, but he begged me to give him my answer right then. His gallantry and decisiveness charmed me, and I happily agreed. A few days later, he told me he wanted to marry me and start a family together. Again I accepted, because I thought I was in love—or at least, in love with his way of expressing himself—and because, although our communication took place over the phone, he was attentive and kind to me. Looking back, I really only fell in love with the *idea* that somebody loved me.

\* \* \*

Four days after he proposed to me, he asked me to go with him to Mexico City. My first answer was no, because I was still in school and didn't want to let my parents down. He responded that he had family members who had college degrees but did not have any money, while he—although he had never gone to college—had a large house, a new car, and more than enough money.

When I still didn't yield, he played the victim, saying I didn't actually love him. I don't know how, but he managed to convince me. He sent me the money to buy a bus ticket, and that very day I set foot in Mexico City for the first time.

My brother didn't know Jorge existed. Actually, nobody did. He was like a ghost that only I had seen. To avoid awkward explanations, I left without telling anybody.

\* \* \*

I don't remember the exact date I got there, but it was in September. It was six in the morning when I arrived at the bus station in Mexico City. Jorge was waiting for me. He was driving a 2006 Cadillac Escalade, the most luxurious of the line. He took me to the Buenavista neighborhood, behind what was known then as the Cuauhtemoc municipality. I didn't find this out until later, but the first house I slept in was part of a mafia of houses known as "the green rooms." These are guarded houses where victims are watched twenty-four hours a day to keep them from fleeing their life of sexual slavery, located in what is informally known as the city's "zone of tolerance," where officials tend to look the other way.

There, at 36 Arista Street, Jorge paid for a room for me. It was a tiny room that contained only a bed, a closet, and a small shelf. After asking me to get settled in, he left. He left me there alone for two days, shut in, under orders to neither leave nor talk to anybody.

He came back the third day and we went out to eat. Close to the room I was staying in, I saw a number of poorly-dressed girls standing around— nearly naked, in fact. Jorge, without any attempt to soften the blow, pointed at the girls and told me I was going to work "like that." I thought he was joking. But that same day he informed me that their destiny was mine as well. I refused, and he, looking like he was about to strike me, instead hit me with the harsh reality. "You have to do what I tell you. If you think I brought you here for any other reason, you are wrong." If I didn't obey him, he told me, he would kill my family.

\* \* \*

I was so afraid. Afraid for my physical wellbeing, for my life, for my family; so I agreed to be sexually exploited by Jorge. It was a bittersweet sensation: I was so terrified, yet at the same time, I felt love for Jorge.

He chose the clothes I would wear for my first night. He taught me how to put on a condom, the positions I should use, and how I should treat the clients. To prove I had learned what he taught me, my exam was rape.

Jorge also chose my name: I was Karen, the new

182

girl on the human trafficking thoroughfare known as Buenavista.

\* \* \*

Jorge gave me my final instructions: a taxi he had called would drop me off on a street corner, and from there I should look for someone named Omar; I was to ask him how much to charge for my services.

Omar was waiting for me inside a hotel. I gave him my fake name, and he took me to a foul-smelling room. There I took off my clothes, put them away, and donned a tiny outfit that was lying on the bed. When I came back out to the street, Omar introduced me to his mother, Alejandra Gil. She assigned me "my corner."

\* \* \*

That night, my hell began. I wept often, because from that moment on, I felt worthless. I would remember my family and how happy I had been with them. I stained the first clients with my blood because the sponge Jorge had given me couldn't contain my menstruation. But the clients didn't care: they kept using me. That first night, more than fifteen men bought me.

I still remember my schedule: Sunday and Monday from 9:00 p.m. to 2:30 a.m.; Tuesday from 10:00 p.m. to 2:30 a.m.; Wednesday from 10:00

p.m. to 3:00 a.m.; Thursday from 10:00 p.m. to 4:00 a.m.; Friday and Saturday from 10:00 p.m. to 6:00 a.m.

It didn't matter if I was on my period or if Jorge had beaten me hours before. Every week I had to hand over 18,000 pesos (about $1000 US) to Jorge. Sometimes, he'd give me 200 pesos for the week, which I used to buy food; other times he wouldn't give me anything. Once, I tried hiding some money to buy myself a can of soda. When he found out, he kicked me until he broke one of my ribs.

\* \* \*

I was exploited for almost two years on the Buena-vista-Sullivan corridor. I would wake up crying. I would cry myself to sleep. I would wake up crying. That was the cycle of my life.

Some clients wanted to force me to take drugs, such as cocaine or crack, and alcohol; others wanted unprotected sex. Some clients got turned on by beating me and others asked me to act like their daughter. They all disgusted me. I've forgotten them all for my mental health.

Only one remains in my head: a man who, while he was taking off his clothes, showed me his gun and badge and told me he was a police officer. How could an authority who should have helped me, have bought me instead?

\* \* \*

Alejandra Gil was my first pimp, but not my only pimp. I also experienced the abuse of Alicia and Dulce. There was little difference. All of them were equally sadistic and had similar rules: I was never to tell anyone that I was being forced to prostitute myself. I was told to say I enjoyed it; I did it out of my own will, because of financial need; I didn't have a pimp. Jorge told me that in case of a raid, I should tell the authorities my grandmother was sick and I needed money for her medicine. It seemed odd to me that they gave so many instructions in case the police came; in the two years I spent being sexually exploited in Sullivan, I never witnessed a raid.

What I did see were girls and women who would arrive for a day or for a season, then I would never see them again. Later I found out why: the human trafficking network Omar and his mother, Alejandra Gil, had knit together extended all the way to New York. One day, they told me to get ready, because they were going to take me out of the country and sell me like some exported merchandise in the United States.

At night I would cry and look for God. "God, why is this happening to me? Help me, and let your will be done." And although my prayers were short, I know God heard me.

The day Jorge was going to take me to a guarded house so he could plan my trip to the northern border, I took advantage of his temporary inattention and hailed a taxi. I hid in a hotel near the Monumento a la Revolución, then moved to another hotel in the historic downtown district. I

185

spent days in hiding, until I finally felt brave enough to go out and file a police report.

That night, as they finished my psychological evaluations, my report triggered a rare scene in the Sullivan neighborhood: a raid took place within the zone of tolerance, and Jorge was arrested. That same night they threw him in the Reclusorio Oriente (East Prison) and I, the following morning, was taken to Fundación Camino a Casa.

\* \* \*

My reintegration process started at Fundación Camino a Casa in 2012. Later, I came under the care of Fundación Reintegra. From there, I continued the legal battle against Jorge and, later, against Alejandra Gil, who disguised herself as a defender of human rights.

During this judicial process, I learned that Jorge wasn't his real name. It was one of the false identities that Saúl Herrera Soriano, a pimp from Tenancingo, Tlaxcala, used to ensnare his victims. Girls like me.

\* \* \*

Saúl Herrera Soriano was sentenced in July 2012 to twenty years in prison for the crime of human trafficking. Another victim also pressed charges, adding another twenty years to his sentence for the crimes he committed against her, for a total of forty years in prison.

Two years later—twenty-four months of lawsuits, investigations, and legal proceedings—justice finally caught up with Alejandra Gil, who described herself as a "sex worker." She supposedly organized HIV prevention workshops and implemented security systems to prevent crimes against prostitutes in the area. Under this pretense, she attended forums and public committee meetings in Congress and the Senate.

However, my story is very different from that of Alejandra Gil, better known as the Madame of Sullivan, who controlled the sex trade on that corridor in Mexico City for thirty years. She would obstruct raids, charge weekly fees to the victims for her own organization, resell condoms that the public health institution gave away for free, and make rounds in her truck to keep everyone supervised and terrified.

\* \* \*

Anyone who knew me when I met Jorge, that summer in 2010, would say I am a different person now. I have dreams. Some I have already accomplished, and others will be fulfilled. The most important thing is that I've recovered my dignity and my freedom.

With the help of Fundación Camino a Casa, Reintegra, and Comisión Unidos vs. Trata, I was able to reunite with my family and obtain my bachelor's degree and then my master's in law at private universities. Since graduating, I've dedicated my professional career to defending other women caught in trafficking networks. One day, they will also be free, and I will be able to support them in their legal processes. I will be a judge or a magistrate, and I will fight the apathy and corruption our country suffers from.

I will be inspired by the best men and women in our society, those who help victims selflessly. I will be inspired, for example, by those who take the time to read these stories. By those who are moved by our suffering and by the love we have received.

And I will fight for other girls like me, as hard as I fought to survive and to have the opportunity to tell you my story.

*To view a Spanish-language video documentary about the experiences of Madaí and the problem of international human trafficking, scan this QR code with your smartphone camera or app.*

# The fine line between trafficking and prostitution

Multiple international committees under the United Nations, the International Labor Organization, and the Organization of American States report that the line between prostitution and sexual exploitation or human trafficking is far too thin.

The special rapporteur for the Human Rights Commission of the United Nations, Sigma Huda, declared in 2016: "For the most part, prostitution as actually practiced in the world usually does satisfy the elements of trafficking.... Thus, State parties with legalized prostitution industries have a heavy responsibility...to ensure that their legalized prostitution regimes are not simply perpetuating widespread and systematic trafficking."[1] It can be shown that, in our world today, countries that have legalized prostitution often do not fulfill this obligation to prevent the perpetuation of human trafficking, something that has been confirmed by several investigations of international relevance.[2]

Prostitution is a well-calibrated machine that is tolerated and accepted due to the perpetuation of myths created by the very population that consumes it, myths that couldn't be further from the truth. It is a group that easily ignores the women who are chained to the system. These gratuitous statements and claims that are used to justify a system of exploitation and pain include:[3,4]

- It is the oldest profession in the world.
- They chose this lifestyle.
- It's just a job like any other.
- It gives women economic independence.
- It is a necessary evil.
- Abolishing prostitution will increase rape.
- Prostitution and human trafficking are two completely different things, and if we criminalize the purchase of sex, the poorest girls in the country will lose great opportunities to move forward.

If we examine each of these statements carefully, we discover they are nothing but myths.

When the sex industry becomes an accepted form of commerce, the myth that male sexuality should be satisfied by the offer of women, girls, and boys available for purchase is affirmed. This necessitates the creation of a group of women whose assault, exploitation, and rape are legitimized, since they are there to supply the demand of the market.[5]

The reality discovered through research and through the testimonies of survivors over the last ten years tells us a very different story: 90% of what appears to be prostitution by choice is actually sexual exploitation.[6] It is not a job like any other, because the violence toward the women involved is intolerable. We might ask ourselves, if prostitution is a choice, why it seems to be reserved for women from poor, uneducated, or indigenous backgrounds or for immigrants.

Dr. Melissa Farley, who has conducted extensive research on this topic, says: "In prostitution, demand creates supply. Because men want to buy sex, prostitution is assumed to be inevitable; therefore it's considered 'normal'."[7] This is a business, an industry in which traffickers and owners of illicit business are the only ones gaining wealth. The annual earnings due to human trafficking for sexual exploitation are ninety-nine billion dollars. This lucrative world requires an entire network of accomplices to achieve its goal, including those who turn a blind eye.[8]

The argument financed by the sex industry, which asserts that prostitution is a right belonging to women who can do whatever they want with their bodies and that legalizing it is the only way to ensure the protection of their labor rights as "sex workers," is an ideological struggle that has plagued the feminist movement. It has been adopted by organizations dedicated to the defense of human rights that disguise themselves as protectors of women but, in reality, serve to perpetuate the sex industry and the crimes that go with it: drug trafficking, money laundering, bribery, corruption, extortion, and especially violence against women, which is the only way to keep providing the "merchandise" to feed the demand.

Those who want to regulate prostitution—or as Julie Bindel calls it, "the pimp lobby," which seeks to normalize prostitution as if it were any other job by using terms such as "sex worker" (a term invented in the eighties by a group of convicted pimps)[9]—justify their arguments by saying women have the right to "the free development of their personalities." In generic terms, this means they have the right to do whatever they want with their bodies; therefore, they have the right to prostitute themselves, and the state has the obligation to protect that right. This opens the door to a philosophical debate that confuses the protection of dignity with the protection of free development of personality. But, when one understands that dignity is an intrinsic part of being human and that all rights emanate from this dignity, especially liberty, which is above all the rest, then it becomes clear that what must be protected, first and foremost, is human dignity.

It is very important to emphasize this distinction. Human beings don't only have the right to be free, they have a right to remain free of all types of slavery or conditions that deprive them of their freedom. This right to remain free of any type of slavery, violence, or other type of inhumane or degrading trade is directly relevant to the crime of human trafficking. Traffickers might attack dignity, but they can't take it away. Dignity is intrinsic to each person and is protected by human rights. Human rights are a legal concept: dignity is a human condition. Trafficking doesn't just violate human rights, it tries to strip its victims of their humanity, that is, their dignity, by transforming them into object or merchandise. Human beings are not objects that lack dignity; we are subjects who possess dignity. From this perspective, any legislation dealing with human trafficking should have, as its judicial focus, the protection of dignity—not the rights that proceed from dignity and are being violated. Therefore, any argument that promotes the legalization of prostitution contains a deep fallacy; plus, it contributes to a measurable increase in human trafficking, it incentivizes sexual tourism, it promotes violence against women, and it enables the expansion of the sexual exploitation industry.[10]

In countries where purchasing sex is illegal, but where, following the equality model, prostituted women are not criminalized (such as Sweden, France, Israel, and Ireland, among others), trafficking rates have been lowered considerably, demonstrating the effectiveness of this model.[11] On the other hand, in countries where legislators have argued that the sex industry is a legitimate business and career path for women (such as the Netherlands, Germany, and New Zealand), the system has failed, and trafficking rates have risen, especially among migrant women and minors. This is because the system encourages pimps and clients to find ways to ensure enough human supply for exploitation—now with the de facto approval of the government, which has removed the legal regulations that hindered pimping, entrapment, and places of prostitution and the businesses that promote this (strip clubs, pornography, virtual sex, massage parlors, and more).

In Mexico, prostitution as such is not regulated, but it is tolerated. Pimping is a crime, but impunity abounds. In the northern zone of Tijuana, an area where we have been working extensively for several years, it is clear that the women are under the control of a pimp or a trafficker. There is no doubt.

The case of Alejandra Gil, mentioned in the story of Madaí, reveals how criminal networks related to the system of prostitution can easily disguise themselves as social activism. In 1985, Alejandra Gil, who called herself a "sex worker," created the civil organization AProSE in order to "protect the labor rights of the sex workers on Sullivan Street" in Mexico City.

The organization claimed to carry out activities and workshops related to the prevention of HIV/AIDS, as well as provide medical attention and implement security measures against violence, homicide, and rape. Gil flew a flag of social justice. She participated in forums and public committee meetings in the Senate and Congress, and she was even recognized by international organizations as a defender of human rights. Even today, there are people within those organizations who raise their voices in her defense.

The testimony of Madaí and another victim, as well as two witnesses, were key in bringing the truth to light and removing her disguise. Gil, the Madame of Sullivan, as she was better known, had controlled the prostitution system on Sullivan Street for thirty years. She was the mastermind behind the exploitation of hundreds of women and girls in that part of the city. As mentioned above, she impeded police raids and ran a surveillance system that controlled the women and informed their pimps if any of them did anything suspicious. Any woman who dared to ask for help received a litany of insults and humiliations. "Move your hips and stay out of problems" was the answer given to Mayra, a victim exploited in Sullivan for sixteen years, when she dared to tell Alejandra about the torture she was suffering from her trafficker.

Gil and her son Omar were finally arrested on February 12, 2014, in the offices of AProSE. There was a great deal of media coverage. The news reporter Adela Micha interviewed Madaí and Gil, allowing the general public to see the reality of sexual exploitation, and she forcefully carried the information straight into the homes of thousands of people. In this case, the media played an important role in bringing the truth to light. After an in-depth investigation, media reported that AProSE had received funds from the federal government totaling around 600,000 pesos for its AIDS prevention programs in 2009 and 172,642 pesos in 2010 for another AIDS prevention program. In 2011 CENSIDA awarded them 250,000 pesos; and the National Social Development Institute awarded a grant of 88,000 pesos for an informative campaign about the papilloma virus. In total, more than one million pesos had been granted in federal funds to this criminal organization.

In 2015, Alejandra Gil and her son Omar Sayun were sentenced to fifteen years in prison. Thanks to the testimony of Madaí and other brave victims, the thirty-year farce of Alejandra Gil, who had acted as the protector of those who "decided" to prostitute themselves, was dismantled.

Many in Mexico fear attempts to discourage the demand for prostitution through laws that criminalize the purchase of sex because they don't want to upset a system so deeply rooted in society. But the reality is that if we don't, we will never be able to decrease the number of women who are exploited to keep it going. It is a new struggle, but it is vital to continue eradicating trafficking in our country and around the world.

Remember, trafficking a person is to infringe on her dignity and on every right that emanates from that dignity, given that it strips the victim of her essence, her human condition, and transforms her into an object. Protecting only the free development of the personality isn't enough. It's useless, even, because you can't defend the personality of someone who is no longer a person, but simply an object. Above all else, her dignity must be protected, and only then can the free development of her personality be protected. Failure to follow this order allows traffickers to claim that the victim "consented" and therefore is free to develop herself however she chooses. Great caution must be exercised because the Palermo Protocol specifically states that consent is not a factor when defining human trafficking. Nobody can consent to being raped, and likewise, nobody can consent to giving up her dignity.

Fighting against trafficking implies defending the dignity of people and all the fundamental human rights that come from it. That means the first cannot be protected if the rest are not defended: human rights cannot exist or be upheld without a prior recognition of dignity.[12]

By definition, dignity is an absolute value, the foundation of human coexistence, the greatest of all values pertaining to freedom, autonomy, equality, and the principles and rights that flow from those values. The idea that prostitution, as it is understood today, is a protection of rights clearly shows many legislators' lack of knowledge regarding the realities that these women experience. Traffickers and owners of illicit businesses take advantage of this ignorance to spread their dangerous and false message. It is time to rise up, to work, to bring the truth to light, and to fight this deception.

# References cited

1.  S. Huda, "Report of the Special Rapporteur on the human rights aspects of the victims of trafficking in persons, especially women and children," The United Nations Comission on Human Rights, February 2016, https://www.refworld.org/docid/48abd53dd.html.
2.  N. Jakobsson and A. Kotsadam, "The law and economics of international sex slavery: prostitution laws and trafficking for sexual exploitation," European Journal of Law and Economics, 35 (1), (2013): 87-107, https://link.springer.com/article/10.1007/s10657-011-9232-0 (Accessed 7-Aug-2017).
3.  European Women's Lobby, "18 Myths on Prostitution," 2013, https://www.womenlobby.org/IMG/pdf/prostitution_myths_final_ewl.pdf.
4.  M. Lamas, Conversation with Marta Lamas [interview with C. Puig], Grupo Milenio, "En 15 con Carlos Puig," Ciudad de México, 3-Feb-2017.
5.  G. Ekberg, "The Swedish Law that Prohibits the Purchase of Sexual Services: Best Practices for Prevention of Prostitution and Trafficking in Human Beings," SAGE journals, 2002, https://doi.org/10.1177/1077801204268647.
6.  Evelina Giobbe, "WHISPER Oral History Project," Minneapolis, Minnesota, 1987, http://www.rapeis.org/activism/prostitution/prostitutionfacts.html (Accessed 12-Sep-2019).
7.  M. Farley and J. Butler, "Prostitution quick facts," 2012, http://www.prostitutionresearch.com/Prostitution%20Quick%20Facts%2012-21-12.pdf (Accessed 12-Sep-2019).
8.  R. Mellado Prince, "Tesis Doctoral: Políticas públicas para desalentar la demanda de explotación sexual en México," Universidad de Baja California, Colima, 2018,

9.  J. Bindel, "The pimping of prostitution," Palgrave McMillan, Londres, RU, 2017.
10. Corte Constitucional Colombiana, Iniciativa equidad de género, "17 intervenciones internacionales a la demanda D0012489," 25-Sep-2018, http://www. corteconstitucional.gov.co/secretaria/.
11. Gunilla S. Ekberg B.S.W., JD, "Briefing on Swedish law and policies on prostitution and trafficking in human beings," 2012, http://www.sccjr.ac.uk/wp-content/ uploads/2012/11/Briefing-Law-and-policies-on-prostitution-and-THB-Sweden-1203082.pdf.
12. Orozco and Mellado-Prince, "Dignidad y libre desarrollo de la personalidad," *El Cotidiano*, Vol 209, Mexico City, May-June 2018, https://issuu.com/elcotidiano/docs/ cotidiano_209 (Accessed 12-Sep-2019).

# Toward a future with dignity

*Every life is* unique and irreplaceable; and yet, the stories of human trafficking share similarities. Most of them begin with a promise and a lie. Women and men, nearly always from vulnerable environments, are deceived by an offer of work, love, or a better life, only to be torn from their world and ultimately exploited.

There are millions of stories of human trafficking that no one has heard, and although they are similar, in each one, a unique life and world are at stake. The Australian organization Walk Free Foundation calculates that every year, 40.3 million men and women are enslaved on this planet. That means that at this moment there are 40.3 million stories that are unknown.[1]

Unfortunately, the majority will not end in hope. That was the case of the first story I heard. I had been invited by the Concerned Women for America to participate in a series of conferences in Washington DC. in 2005, and it was there that I first became acquainted with the subject. I heard the story of Danguolè Rasalaitè, who inspired the movie *Lilya 4-ever,* directed by Lukas Moodysson. Danguolè was a young Lithuanian victim of sex trafficking. After she managed to escape, she chose to end her life by jumping from a bridge in Sweden, the country where she had been enslaved. She was sixteen years old.

The story left a deep impact on me. After the training, I returned to Mexico determined to help the survivors of this awful crime reintegrate into society—but I couldn't find them. At the time, there was no law in Mexico that penalized human trafficking according to the Protocol to Prevent, Suppress and Punish Trafficking in Persons, especially Women and Children, which complemented the United Nations Convention against International Organized Crime, also known as the Palermo Protocol, and other international conventions signed by Mexico.

The authorities weren't trained to identify victims, and because of this, there were no organized efforts to rescue them. If the problem itself is not understood, what chance is there that survivors will be found?

For that reason, in 2007 we opened Fundación Camino a Casa, the first shelter specializing in human trafficking victims in Mexico. That is how we started our fight, by assisting minors rescued from sex trafficking. Over time, the cause led us to get more and more involved. We've learned over the years that in order to reintegrate the victims, we need laws and legal frameworks that encourage the filing of police reports and indictments, facilitate raids and rescue operations, and ultimately bring about justice. Along with that, society itself must become aware that, rather that stigmatizing the victims, we must show solidarity with them.

Because the reintegration of the victims is our constant focus, we have promoted the prevention of this type of crime with society at large, working in public and political arenas to promote the drafting and creation of adequate laws, the training and education of authorities at all levels, and even the development of processes for restorative justice with convicted traffickers.

We want to share what we've learned from more than a decade of involvement and commitment. We believe our experience can be valuable for anyone, anywhere in the world, who wants to help the survivors of modern-day slavery. This book is a collection of stories that survivors have shared with us, survivors who have received assistance from Fundación Camino a Casa, Reintegra Mexico, Reintegra USA, Rescue Freedom, Unlikely Heroes, and dozens of other organizations connected through Comisión Unidos vs. Trata (United vs. Trafficking Commission).

The first reintegration model, created by Fundación Camino a Casa, is a long-term project, financed by civil organizations in Mexico, that assists victims of human trafficking as they reintegrate into society. This helps in the fulfillment of Article

6.3 of the Palermo Protocol, which states that "Each State Party shall consider implementing measures to provide for the physical, psychological and social recovery of victims of trafficking in persons, including, in appropriate cases, in cooperation with non-governmental organizations, other relevant organizations and other elements of civil society."[2]

Around the world, and in most government-operated shelters, victims of trafficking receive attention for a period of three to six months. They are often placed together with survivors of other crimes, which means they do not receive specialized attention and, in many cases, can create an environment of stigmatization.

Women who are victims of sex trafficking often face double or triple discrimination based on gender stereotypes, since they are judged to be "bad women," "promiscuous," or "dangerous." This hinders the reintegration process, because it produces more violence toward the victims. A shelter must be a place free from revictimization for survivors, because more than anything, they need to focus on building and caring for their self-esteem and protecting their dignity as human beings with rights.

We have observed that the victims, having been sexually abused fifteen to thirty times a day for months or years, come to the shelter completely devastated, with no will to live, full of anger and hatred toward everybody. This forces us to ask ourselves: "Can the breath of life be recovered after the suffering of human trafficking?" The answer is clear: in an understanding and loving environment where the integrity and dignity of people are safeguarded, and where survivors receive care and attention that protect and fully respect their human rights, *it is possible.*

This book is intended to show how out of this traumatic, illegal, devastating experience can come an opportunity to reinvent oneself with the support of others. Of course, the physical, emotional, and psychological scars from human trafficking cannot be remedied in a matter of months, like most governments believe. Usually it takes many years, as we have discovered in our work. This is the main reason we believe in a specialized, long-term model.

It should be added that human trafficking is an injustice provoked by other injustices. That is, a human trafficking victim, before being trafficked, is often already a victim of poverty, violence, discrimination, and other social ills. The "National Diagnosis on the Situation of Human Trafficking in Mexico," in 2014, identified 363 municipalities where the population, especially the women, live in conditions of high vulnerability to human trafficking, and 464 municipalities with medium vulnerability. The areas of high danger are concentrated in the south-southeast region, the border zones of Chihuahua, Sinaloa, and Sonora; and the borders between Jalisco, Nayarit, and Durango.[3]

The diagnosis goes on to say that this vulnerability is due to high illiteracy levels, low employment levels, precarious working conditions, high rates of marginalization and poverty, and constant, high immigration flow.

Prior to their slavery, survivors were already suffering cycles of revictimization that cannot easily be broken. Does it make sense to care for a victim for three months and then return her to the same place and the same conditions as before, only for her to be caught again? That would be like abandoning her midway; in many cases, she would be returning to the accomplices of her victimizers, with no means to build a new life, often cut off from continuing her legal processes.

Only a long-term reintegration model—which in our experience has extended, in some cases, longer than eight years—can break these cycles. The psychological attention and legal accompaniment are complemented by education and work training. Besides working to cure the wounds caused by trafficking (in other words, working on the past), we are concerned about the future: that survivors would truly become autonomous individuals, free from codependent relationships.

The "book of dreams," a dynamic we have adopted to work with survivors on their life plan, illustrates this goal. When they arrive at the shelter, they generally do not have dreams because they have been subjected to a daily routine of terror. As we pointed out above, we want them to recover their lives and their emotional and physical integrity, which we believe (and have seen firsthand) involve the capacity to dream, to look to the future, and to have the strength to live in hope.

In the book of dreams, they write out their goals and desires for their new lives. These blank pages become filled with writing as they walk through their healing process. We have witnessed the crystallization of many of these dreams. We have watched with pride how these girls, boys, women, and men recover their voice and their will, and how they claim their place in the world.

This is a long process and—it must be pointed out—an expensive one. The lack of funding to combat human trafficking and to aid the victims has been a constant reality in Mexico. As of the date of publication of this book in Spanish, the "Fund for the Protection and Assistance toward Victims of Crimes in Matters of Human Trafficking," created by our 2012 law, remains empty. This has never paralyzed us. Relying solely on resources from the civil sector, without any financial support from government programs, Fundación Camino a Casa has served over two hundred survivors, and the Comisión Unidos vs. Trata has served over one hundred more.

In the face of criminal violence and government inaction, civil society must respond with solidarity. Death must be countered with life. We believe there is an ethical motive that makes all citizens, especially those who enjoy their full rights, responsible for fighting for those who have been oppressed.

I come from a privileged home, but one that was

built on effort and work. My father overcame poverty to became one of the most successful men in his profession. He did not have an education past middle school, but by selling door-to-door and office-to-office, he was able to prosper. My father always told me that with effort and the guidance of others, all people can achieve their dreams.

Thanks to his work, as a child I lived in one of the most exclusive residential areas of Mexico City. I traveled and lived abroad. I received the best education he could give me. And more importantly, I had a mother and father who loved each other, who in just a few months will celebrate sixty-three years of marriage. They both taught me to love and respect the dignity of others; they taught me that often the only thing people need in order to shine is a friendly hand.

As if that were not enough, I married the son of a mechanic who became a champion in the insurance and securities industries. He is an extraordinary husband and has supported me financially from the beginning in this fight against trafficking. Alex is a man I admire because he outdoes himself every day, and he loves God and others with deeds, not just with words. Our thirty-six years of marriage have been very happy.

I mention my life story because my participation in the fight against trafficking should not be understood as an act of goodness, but rather as an act of responsibility. All of us who have been given opportunities must fight so that others may have them too. All of us who have received love must give it as well.

People from the Jewish community have long supported us in this fight. I learned from Alberto Kibrit that *tzedeká,* the Hebrew word used for a donation, is the word *justice.* Giving is an act of justice. We must do justice, and that means doing our part so that the rights of the most vulnerable are finally respected. We give so that those who have been deprived will receive what they are due.

The world urgently needs justice. According to the Oxfam International Confederation's report titled "An Economy for the 99%," eight individuals possess the same wealth as 3.6 billion people, the poorest half of humanity.[4] This data suggests that the current economic system is only benefiting the most wealthy. It's not a coincidence that this is the era of human history with the most slaves. That is why, as Oxfam says, we must build a more human economy. We must end the system that's been built on accumulation and objectification, where greed reigns with its desire for wealth and power at the cost of others.

Although this sounds impossible, and some might call us naive, a new world can begin to be built out of the sum of our collective wills. What can you do for others? How much are you willing to give?

These questions have been asked by every professional, woman, man, psychologist, lawyer, social worker, volunteer, and companion who has participated in our commitment to a long-term care model for trafficking victims. That is why the model we have designed is not based on hope, but on solidarity. Hope establishes vertical relationship where the one who gives is above the one who is receiving. We seek horizontal relationships, where everyone who is involved is equal. It is worth mentioning that in this we are recognizing the inherent complexity in the processes of giving and receiving.

In June 2017, the Malta Summit, organized by the Pontifical Academy of Sciences, The Amersi Foundation, and the Presidency Foundation for the Welfare of Society, addressed models and best practices to eradicate modern slavery and restore the dignity of the victims. The Mexican civil model for victims of sexual exploitation was recognized publicly, and other countries were urged to study and adopt it.[5] Given the responsibility that this recognition implies, we are putting into the hands of the world our experience, our learning over the years, our story. This is the heart of our model and, therefore, of this book.

As Germán Villar, founder of Reintegra Mexico (a project now headed by Andy McCullough and his team after Germán's passing) often said, "We are not trying to change the lives of the survivors: they are the ones changing us." We do not attempt to dictate how the survivors must live. We want to accompany them, walking by their side, so that they—and only they—make the final decisions for their lives.

# References cited

1.  Walk Free Foundation, "Global Slavery Index 2018," https://www.globalslaveryindex.org/2019/findings/executive-summary/ (Accessed 4-Sep-2019).
2.  United Nations Treaty Collection, "The Protocol to Prevent, Suppress and Punish Trafficking in Persons, especially Women and Children," https://treaties.un.org/doc/source/RecentTexts/18-12-a.S.htm (Accessed 13-Sep-2019).
3.  United Nations Office on Drugs and Crime, "Diagnóstico Nacional sobre la situación de trata de personas en México," México: Secretaría de Gobernación, 2014, https://www.unodc.org/documents/mexicoandcentralamerica/Diagnostico_trata_de_personas.pdf (Accessed 4-Sep-2019).
4.  Deborah Hardoon, "Es hora de construir una economía más humana y justa al servicio de las personas," Oxfam International, 16-Jan-2012, https://www.oxfam.org/es/informes/una-economia-para-el-99 (Accessed 4-Sep-2019).
5.  The Pontifical Academy of Science, "Malta summit: Sharing models and best practices to end modern slavery and restore dignity to its victims," http://www.pas.va/content/dam/accademia/booklet/booklet_malta.pdf (Accessed 12-Sep-2019).

# We need your help

One of the most important steps for the survival of this program is to widen the support network through individuals, educational institutions, businesses, and organizations. Without this network, it would be impossible to accompany survivors over the long term, until they reach the goals they themselves have written on their blank page. Today we are directly supporting sixty-nine survivors in shelters and halfway programs. You can make a great difference in their lives from your place of influence.

We invite you to join this great cause by making a donation through our websites:

www.comisionunidos.org
www.fundacioncaminoacasa.org

You can also make a deposit or transfer into our bank account in Mexico.

Comisión Unidos vs. Trata A.C.
Banamex branch 7002
Account number: 8343173
CLABE: 002180700283431737
SWIFT: BNMXMXMM

Thank you so much for your support.
Together we make all the difference.

# Acknowledgments

*The only thing necessary for the triumph of evil is for good men to do nothing.*
—Edmund Burke

*Never doubt that a small group of thoughtful, committed citizens can change the world; indeed, it's the only thing that ever has.*
—Margaret Mead

As they say, "silent gratitude doesn't do anyone any good." In that spirit, I would like to thank so many wonderful people who have saved valuable lives; who have given them a blank page to restart their dreams and their goals; who have accompanied the victims on the reintegration path until they have become brave survivors, reflections of a light that proves *success is possible* after the hell of human trafficking.

I would like to thank my parents, who filled me with love since I was born and taught me how valuable every person is, how important gratitude is, how to fight for our convictions, and that recognition is better than criticism.

To my family for what I learn from you every day and for your constant support.

If we want to move forward in the task of rescuing valuable lives and bringing criminals to justice, we must mention those who have taken effective actions: rescuing victims, opening shelters, seeking justice, carrying out prevention campaigns, and closing illegal businesses. The sad truth is that few people are actually doing something, which is why it is so important to name and to thank those who are or have exercised their influence and authority without special interests or fears.

There are many people on this path who have shown that empathy is possible and who deserve thanks in return; and yet, since there are so many who have joined us on this journey at one moment or another, I can't mention everyone. Here, however, is a brief list:

My dear Alex, my companion, friend, lover, and partner against trafficking: there aren't enough words to express my gratitude; you have never limited me, rather you have supported unconditionally my commitment to help victims with all you have. Only God knows the price you have paid. You are the best partner and the best husband in the world.

To Rita Hernandez: for your invaluable friendship, for all your contributions to Comisión Unidos vs. Trata, for personally giving the survivors a blank page, and for your extraordinary collaboration on this book. Thank you very much, my dear Lion.

To Oscar Balderas: the love you have shown to each survivor is unique; you have used your talents to write the best about each of them.

Blank Page became a social movement in support of trafficking victims thanks to Clemente Cámara, whom I acknowledge for your years of support; but especially for a transcendent meeting with Karla Jacinto and Zunduri, where they concluded that this would be the best way to explain their story, their new birth.

Many thanks to Justin and Angela Jaquith for blessing my family and for the hours spent dedicated to our book, *Blank Page*.

Thank you to Mike and Cindy Jacobs for your love and valuable advice.

I value the friendship, support, and advice from Denzel and Becky Hood, Andrés and Mayita Castelazo, Andrés and Kelly Spyker, and the whole family and team of Cash and Sonia Luna.

To the CASA family that has always been an example of love and solidarity.

To the incredible team of Comision Unidos vs. Trata: you are the best example of perseverance, generosity, and love.

Thank you, Ruth Gómez for your guidance; thank you, Liliana Banegas, Miguel Sierra, Paty González, Karla Jacinto, Ernesto and Elba Bautista, Gaby Morales, Esperanza and Enrique, Evelyn Gutiérrez, Graciela and Ricardo, Miriam, Esther Escobar, Marlene Maya, Claudia Valeria, Andrey Ibarra, Nayeli Plata, Raul Ramiréz, and Nina Corona.

Thank you to the council chaired by Armando Culebro and Lucy Chaparro. Special thanks for all the time you have invested in Comisión Unidos vs. Trata.

I am always grateful for the work done by the Pontifical Academy of Social Science in the Vatican through Chancellor Marcelo Sánchez Sorondo, Gaby Marino, and the wonderful team that has contributed more to the world than any other organization. In Mexico, to Alfonso Miranda, Carlos Aguiar, Francisco Robles, Manuel Corral, and Alfredo Quintero.

I admire and learn from each of the people who lead organizations within the Coalition for the Abolition of Prostitution (CAP), and I especially thank our friends Gregoire Thery and Dianne Matte, who head the coalition.

To the people who work tirelessly in Fundación Camino a Casa, especially Patricia Prado de Caso, who achieved the best model of reintegration and has donated her time, money, and effort since 2007.

220

Eternally grateful to Germán Villar† and Lorena Argueta, of Reintegra; Andy and Robin McCullough and Rich and Brenda Lotteries, of Reintegra USA; Erica Graves of Unlikely Heroes; Del Chitin and Jeremy Vallerand, of Rescue Freedom; and Tim Ballard of Operation Underground Railroad.

To all the GSN friends chaired by Raza Jafar.

To Claudia Lizaldi, Martha and Lizeth Sáenz for starting the sponsorship.

To Robert Morris and Jacobo Ramos of Gateway Church.

Very special thanks to Alberto and Naty Kibrit, Rafael Avante, Rani Hong, and the team of Freedom Seal Mexico.

To my dear Mariana Ruenes and the whole team from @SINTRATA, who love and support survivors with actions.

To each of my neighbors who created a chat group to support survivors and be available to meet day-to-day needs.

Special thanks to Olga Sánchez Cordero, Alejandro Encinas, Santiago Nieto, Aaron Mastache, Miguel Ángel Mancera, Eruviel Ávila, Rubén Moreira, Alfredo Del Mazo, Marco Mena, Ignacio Peralta, Francisco García Cabeza de

Vaca, Claudia Sheinbaum, Margarita Zavala, Manuel Velasco, Alejandro Gomez, Dilcya García Espinosa of the Monteros, Rodrigo Espeleta, Gabriel O'Shea, Santiago Ramos Millán, Maribel Cervantes, Oscar Valdes, Sergio Chavelas, Luis Cardenas, Melissa Vargas, Jacqueline Garcia, Isabel Sánchez, Angela Quiroga, Mikel Arriola, Guillermina Cabrera, Juana \ Camila Bautista, Manelich Castilla, Raciel López, Rubén Vasconcelos, José Antonio Aquiahuatl, Oscar Montes de Oca, José Ramón Amieva, Irving Barrios, Edmundo Garrido, Rodrigo De la Riva, Angels Dorantes, Rafael War, Ernestina Godoy, Sergio Medina, Leticia Varela, Nancy De La Sierra, Anita Sánchez, Manuel Añorve, Nelly Montealegre, Adriana Lizarraga, Claudia Pérez, Mariana Rodríguez, Adrián Rubalcava, Ernesto Millán, and Kenya López.

Today we have a Ley vs. Trata (Law vs. Trafficking) that makes it possible to have 99% of the traffickers of the victims we have served in prison, thanks to my fellow legislators in the LXI Legislature and to those who faithfully refused to allow setbacks: Julieta Fernández Márquez, Leticia López Landeros, Paola Félix Díaz, Fernando De las Fuentes Hernández, José Alfredo Ferreiro Velazco, Pablo Escudero Morales, Hugo Eric Flores Cervantes, Jesús Sesma Suárez, Raúl Cervantes Andrade, and Silvana Beltrones Sánchez.

Thank you to all the organizations, the lawyers, and the activists and counselors of Unidos vs. Trata who did not allow changes to be made to the Ley vs. Trata that would have benefited the traffickers, and/or who support the victims.

Special thanks to Karla De la Cuesta, Luis Gallego, Patricia Olamendi, Aaron Lara, Ferdinando Recio, Luis Wertman, Adriana De la Source, Andrés Simg, Adan and Laura Bernal, Marisol Sosa, Martha Torres, Clemente Cámara, Sylvia Sánchez Alcántara, Verónica Salame, Raul Arias, Alma Rosa Lugo, Bruno Alarcón, Eduardo Achach, Emília Reyes, Nieves Fernández, Avelino and Marisol González, Gonzalo and Virginia Espina, Jony Vázquez, Laura Herrejon, Tito Quiroz, Erika Cortés, Laura Ponce, Lety Mora, Alex and Elizabeth Martínez, Juan Manuel Estrada, José Manuel Sánchez, Raúl Camou, Mariana Villalbazo, Narciso Hernández, Patrícia Yun, Pia De Vecchi, Rodrigo Moreno, José Luis Ayoub, Ayla Merino, Victoria Hernández, Alejandro Marti, Joaquín Quintana, Julio Malvido, Brenda Rosales, Sophie Hayes, Adriana Páramo, Nelly Jimenez O'Farrill, Gina Diez Barroso, Sarah Bustani, Ana La Salvia, Beatriz Mendivil, Alejandra Ambosi, Ernestina Sodi, Sergio Castillo, Alberto and Trixia Valle, Gerardo Fernández Noroña, Linda Shaw, Andi Buerger, Blanquita Cullum, Verónica Flores, Orlando Camacho, Isabel Miranda, Bernardo Noval, Victor

Hugo Martin, Efrén Ruiz, Tanya Moss, René and
Lorena Villar, Gilberto and Monica Urzúa,
Gustavo and Nancy López, Cesar Daniel and
Colibrí Gonzalez, Tere Madruga, Jorge Olvera,
Manuel Elizondo, Samuel González, Tere Paredes,
Andrés Naime, Elias Huerta, Jorge Garcia
Villalobos, Mabel Lozano, Luis Rosales, Raúl
López Infante, Cuauhtémoc Ibarra, Hector Pérez,
Nuria Hernández Abarca, Patricia Olamendi,
Bhavook, Mariah, Siya Tripathi, Hugo Scherer,
Tony Schiena, Lina Kouatly, Blanquita Cullum,
Lynn Shaw, Andrea Lafferty, Michael and Carol
Hart, Mauricio and Virginia Ruiz, Armando and
Martha Alducin, Rebeca Bremer, Norma Ruiz,
Diana Aristizabal, Hornung Family, Hugo and
Tati Martínez, Arvi Cruz, Carlos Quiroa, Mike
Reyes, Dann Quero, Seth Jafet, Cristian Vélez,
Alan Fernando, Joe and Becky Keenan, José and
Michel Mayorquin, María Sorté, Rodrigo and
Yuri, Rubén Manríquez, Ricardo Del Valle,
Antonio Salinas, Lidia Nistor Reteneller,
Marianela Mina, Family Castellanos, Susana
Peressutti, Lorena Martins, Gustavo Vera,
Gustavo Espinosa, Manuel Elizondo, José
Fernández de Cevallos, Adriana and Alfonso
Hernández, Ana Bertha and Alex López, Alma
Delia and José Luis López, Mayra Rivera, Liebano
and Tata Sáenz, Carlos and Esther Rivera, Marce
and Christofer Olvera, Claudia and Javier Vargas,
Claudia and Omar Dergal, Hydrangea and Daniel
Serrano, Luciana and David Rodríguez, Mariana

and Emilio Balcázar, Evita and Enrique Pineda,
Ericka and Jesús Delgado, Marce and Fernando
Urrea, Jenny Anduaga, Jéssica Torreslanda, Julia
and José Serrano, Lau and Raul Hernández, Lily
and Alex Carpinteiro, Luciana and Paco Soto,
Naty and Chuy García, Miguel and Vero Cantero,
Silvia and Rolando Espinosa, Galdina Sáenz, Lety
Cordoba, Lucy Zezatti, Raquel and Ricardo
Pineda, Ángeles and Juan Manuel Soriano, Carla
and Ricardo García, Estelita and Luis Marín,
Perla and Jorge Ramírez, Mimi and Gustavo
Hernández, Karla and Sergio Espín, Esperanza
Terán, Lourdes and Bernie Saldivar, Martha and
Toño Mandujano, and Ramsés Herrera.

To Lupita, Angie, Jazmín, and Paola.

To the Red de Refugios vs. Trata (Network of
Shelters against Trafficking) and all the people
who every day help them rebuild the course of
their lives and dream again, with a blank age in
front of them: Iliana Ruvalcaba, Mariana
Wenzel, Adan Duncan, Alma Tucker, Claudia
Colimoro, Elsa Simón Ortega, Ernesto and Elba
Bautista, Liliana Banegas, Mother Maria Marcela,
Mayra Hernández, Sofía Almazan, Trini Delgado,
Nury Reyes, Sandra Diéguez, and Irma Mejía. You
perform the most important and difficult work in
the fight against human trafficking. You have my
full admiration.

To each and every member of the media that has given a voice to the survivors and activists. Especially Adela Micha, Adriana Páramo, Adriana Pérez Cañedo, Agustin Ceruso, Alejandra Aguayo, Alejandro Cacho López, Alejandro Maldonado, Alejandro Pacheco, Alfonso Clara, Alfredo Villeda, Alicia Salgado, Álvaro Carmona, Amadeo Lara, Beloved Avendaño, Amical Salazar, Ana María Lomelí, Ana María Salazar, Ana Paula Ordorica, Andrea Merlo, Andrea Mireles, Arturo Ortíz Mayen, Azucena Uresti, Bárbara Barquín, Bibiana Belsasso, Blanca Lolve, Blanca Valadez, Bogdán Castillo, Carlos Aguilar, Carlos Loret de Mola, Carlos Marín, Carlos Puig, Carmen Aristegui, Ciro Di Costanzo, Claudia Arellano, Daisy Paniagua, Danielle Dithurbide, Daniel Flores, David Fuentes, Deena Graves, Edmundo Velázquez, Eduardo Ávila, Eduardo Ramos Fusther, Eduardo Ruíz Healy, Efrén Argüelles, Elisa Salinas, Emma Hernández, Enrique Davis, Enrique Muñoz, Erika de la Luz, Erika Araujo, Estela Livera, Evangelina Hernández, Federico Lamont, Federico Vale Castilla, Fernanda Familiar, Fernanda Tapia, Flor de Luz Osorio Ruiz, Francisco Fortuño, Francisco Garfias, Francisco Zea, Francesca Salinas, Francine Sarrapy Fabre, Gabriela Lara, Gabriela Warketin, Georgina Baltazar, Guadalupe Vallejo, Héctor de Mauleón, Hena Cuevas, Humberto Padgett, Ignacio Anaya, Isaac Ajzen, Isabel Posadas, Ivonne Arriaga, Jaime Núñez Piña, Janett Arceo Maldonado, Jesús Martín Mendoza, Joel Aguirre, Jorge Fernández Meléndez,

Jorge Zarza Pineda, Jorge Armando Rocha, José Antonio López, José Cárdenas Vizcaíno, José Luis Arévalo, Juan Antonio Jiménez, Juan Francisco Rocha, Judith Miguel, Julián Andrade, Karla Iberia Sánchez, Kimberly Armengol, Leonardo Curzio, Leopoldo Mendívil, Lilly Téllez, Lydiette Carreón, Lolita Vega, Lourdes Mendoza, Lorena Morales, Luis Cárdenas, Luis Chaparro, Manuel Santa Ana, Margarita Rodriguez, Mariana Braun, Maribel Carrillo, Mariela Castañón, Mario Torres, Martha Reyes, Martha Debayle, Maxi Pelaez, Monica Garza, Neyra Moncayo, Nino Canún, Nora Patricia Jara López, Oscar Mario Beteta, Pablo Hiriart, Pamela Cerdeira, Pamela Zazueta, Paola Rojas Hinojosa, Pedro Ferriz Hijar, Pepe Vega, Porfirio Patiño, Rafael Romo, Raúl Flores, Raúl García Araujo, Raymundo Rivapalacio, Ricardo Rocha, Roberto Avilés Vázquez "Callo de hacha", Roberto Rock, Rocío Marfil, Ruffo, Rufino Irineo, Salvador García Soto, Santos Mondragón, Selene Ávila, Sofía Sánchez Navarro, Témoris Grecko, Tirma Pérez Escudero, Tristán Canales, Vanessa Job, Victor Hugo Acevedo, Victor Hugo Michel, Víctor Trujillo "Brozo", Yazmil Jalil, and Yohali Resendiz.

To our detractors and opponents with regard to human trafficking: thank you, because so many activists and fighters have risen up, and we have been able to bring out the best in ourselves.

To you, the government official who has given your support to the subject of rescuing the dignity of trafficking survivors, all my recognition and gratitude.

To each and every one of the activists and survivors who today share their stories to prevent trafficking, thank you for what you have allowed us to learn; I admire you. Thank you for thinking about others who could fall into the same trap or who need to be rescued. We are sure that your stories will move people's hearts.

To you, who have supported with donations, with publications, with work, with your valuable time: thank you, a million times over; but there is still more to do.

# About the author

**Rosi Orozco** is a tireless activist who has been working toward the prevention of human trafficking crimes for over fourteen years. Her message has reached millions of people around the world, and she has had particular success in reintegrating victims of this crime into society. Rosi has dedicated herself to the promotion and defense of human rights through various associations. Since 2005, she has specialized in strategies to prevent and combat human trafficking. She has worked with over three hundred survivors, making sure they receive personalized support and care according to their needs.

In 2009, as a legislator in the House of Representatives of Legislature LXI, she promoted the General Law against this crime, which has had far-reaching results in advancing the fight against trafficking. Rosi has written four books, and because of her efforts she has received national and international recognition; although carrying out this work has also put her life in danger on innumerable occasions.

It is the human trafficking survivors who push Rosi to continue fighting to achieve a Mexico free from this crime. Rosi believes, "Together we can make all the difference—and we already are."

**Rosi Orozco:**
Instagram @Rosi_Orozco
Facebook Rosi Orozco
Twitter @rosiorozco

Comisión Unidos vs. Trata:
@unidosvstrata
www.comisionunidos.org

Fundación Camino a Casa:
@fcaminoacasa
www.fundacioncaminoacasa.org

# About the contributor

*Rita María Hernández* is a wife, mother, and grandmother. She has a master's degree in education sciences and a PhD in public policy from the University of Baja California with a specialty in counseling for women, teenagers, and girls. She has worked for thirty-five years in the educational field, running educational centers, writing curriculum, and training leaders. For ten years, she has worked on issues related to sex trafficking and violence against women and girls.

From 2015 to 2018, she worked as Director of Comisión Unidos vs. Trata, where she still collaborates. Today, she is the general director of HPA Educational Services, a member of the executive committee of the International Coalition for the Abolition of Prostitution, president of the organization Por Siempre Libre (Forever Free) in Tijuana, and general director of Mujer Libre (Free Woman), an online ministry for women. She was the winner of the Human Rights award in 2017 in Baja California granted by the State Human Rights Commission.

If you agree that victims deserve a new story and a new chance, take a picture with a blank sheet of paper, tag it with our hashtag, #HojaEnBlanco, and post, tag, or send it to:

**@unidosvstrata** *Twitter*
**Unidos vs. Trata** *Facebook*
**unidosvstrata** *Instagram*

Join the movement
# #HojaEnBlanco

Report human trafficking and other crimes anonymously through *Crime Stoppers International.* anonymousreporting.org

Made in the USA
Middletown, DE
18 December 2023